The Progressive Education Movement

Is It Still a Factor in Today's Schools?

William Hayes

Rowman & Littlefield Education
Lanham • New York • Toronto • Plymouth, UK
2006

Published in the United States of America
by Rowman & Littlefield Education
A Division of Rowman & Littlefield Publishers, Inc.
A wholly owned subsidary of The Rowman & Littlefield Publishing Group, Inc.
4501 Forbes Boulevard, Suite 200, Lanham, Maryland 20706
www.rowmaneducation.com

Estover Road
Plymouth PL6 7PY
United Kingdom

British Library Cataloguing in Publication Information Available

Library of Congress Cataloging-in-Publication Data

Hayes, William, 1938–
  The progressive education movement : is it still a factor in today's schools? /
William Hayes.
     p. cm.
  Includes bibliographical references.
  ISBN-13: 978-1-57886-521-5 (cloth : alk. paper)
  ISBN-13: 978-1-57886-522-2 (pbk. : alk. paper)
  ISBN-10: 1-57886-521-2 (cloth : alk. paper)
  ISBN-10: 1-57886-522-0 (pbk. : alk. paper)
  1. Progressive education—United States—History. 2. Education—United
States—Philosophy. 3. Student-centered learning—United States. I. Title.
  LB1027.3.H39 2007
  370.11—dc22   2006020729

Contents

Foreword

As a student in the late 1960s, I took an alternative route to becoming a teacher. I did not take the traditional teacher education courses that so many of my contemporaries had taken. Instead, I took a smorgasbord of courses in literature, history, economics, geography, political science, and religion. These were infused with a steady diet of social commentary and readings such as *The Open Classroom* (Herbert Kohl), *Death At An Early Age* (Jonathan Kozol), *The Geranium On The Window Just Died But Teacher You Went Right On* (Albert Cullum), and *Teaching As A Subversive Activity* (Neil Postman and Charles Weingartner). Those, I later learned, were writings reflecting progressive education and the thinking of John Dewey and other progressive philosophers and educators. As I began teaching, I often heard Dewey and other progressive thinkers spoken about with either great ardor or great disdain, depending on the politics and worldview of the speaker.

Some saw Dewey and the progressives as the humanizing and saving force in an educational world of conformity, bureaucratic assumptions, and impersonal approaches to teaching and learning. Here at last was a student-centered approach that honored children's playful and naturally curious qualities. Experiential learning, real world problem solving, and discovery-focused education were the calls to order. Progressive educators saw such approaches to teaching and learning as natural and necessary ingredients in a democracy, ones that were essential to a democracy's survival and growth.

The other perceptions regarding progressive education that I often encountered suggested an alternative perspective. Some viewed progressive education as "all that is wrong with our children, schools, and society today." A belief by many had arisen that a rampant individualism and a child-centered approach in our schools were contributing to, among other things, a lack of discipline, a decline in content mastery, and a loss of regard for authority and tradition. A decline in patriotism and respect for our national icons were also laid at the feet of progressive educators. Some suggested that progressive child-raising techniques coupled with progressive education had given rise to a weakened family structure, loss of respect for religious traditions, and an unhealthy questioning of authority.

Of course, as is often the case, I discovered the truth about these contentious issues was found somewhere in between the poles of rhetoric. There were few examples of "pure practices" within either camp. Project-oriented learning without requisite knowledge and skills often led to chaos and less than meaningful end results in classrooms. Cross-disciplinary and whole-child approaches to instruction were exciting, stimulating, and productive. They were also time-consuming, relied on system-wide support, and forced difficult decisions about what to leave out of an ever-expanding curriculum. The "either/or" conundrum did not work for me or many of my colleagues as we struggled to find our teaching philosophies and approaches to classroom instruction. Rather, infusing and integrating aspects of progressive education while confronting the realities of public schooling and its accompanying bureaucratic tendencies seemed to become the norm for many educators of my generation.

Where are we today with increasing calls for standards and standardization, accountability and high-stakes testing, and increasing state and federal mandates? William Hayes, an educator whose career has spanned much of this time period and who has dealt with these issues as a classroom teacher, school administrator, college professor, parent, and active community member, takes us on a journey through the history of progressive education from its inception up to the present-day dilemmas facing our society. In *The Progressive Education Movement: Is It Still A Factor In Today's Schools?* he explores the role of progressive education in many of the key movements and events in public schooling in the twentieth century. Hayes also challenges us to consider the future of progressive education in today's political and cultural climate. These are important and useful questions for educators, parents, and citizens of a democracy to seriously consider.

Peter W. Knapp Ed. D.
Associate Professor of Education
Roberts Wesleyan College

Acknowledgments

For this my tenth book, I am deeply indebted to two student workers in our Teacher Education Division office. Chelsea Durham is a senior who has worked with me on three books during her years here at the college. This year being her senior year, she has spent one semester student teaching, making it necessary to have the additional assistance of sophomore Julia Clark. These students have helped in every phase of this project from the research to final proofreading. They are outstanding young people who will themselves become leaders in their chosen profession. Finally, I will forever be grateful to my wife, Nancy, who proofread every page in all of the books. Her work through the years has always greatly improved the final products. As important has been her support and patience. Without these three individuals, this book would not have been possible.

Introduction

For some time now, I have accepted the idea that a major theme in the history of education in the United States during the past century has been the ongoing debate between those who consider themselves traditionalists and those who espouse the principles of progressive education. For me, this idea was highlighted in an article that appeared in the *Education Digest* in April 1999. In the "Top 10 Education Events of the 20th Century," the author, Ben Brodinsky, lists such events as the development of public schools, standardized tests, and the mandating of special education for handicapped children. One of his topics was called "Innovative Thoughts." In describing this part of our history, he points to the impact of John Dewey in introducing what has been labeled progressive education.[1]

Although few would question the impact of progressive education, actually defining the specific objectives and methods advocated by the reform movement is difficult. In her book *Left Back: A Century of Battles over School Reform*, respected conservative historian Diane Ravitch refers to Herbert M. Kliebard's view that progressive education "covered such a broad range of different, even contradictory, ideas that it was a meaningless term." In the same paragraph, Ravitch admits that many other educational historians, such as Lawrence A. Cremin, saw a pattern of beliefs that allows one to give meaning to the movement.[2]

Certainly many writers have attempted to articulate the difference between the traditional approach to education and that which is put forward by the progressives. Unfortunately, such comparisons are often tainted by the prejudices of the author. For instance, a recent attempt at comparing the two philosophies included the following contrasts. In the area related to curriculum, the author writes that with the traditional or classical approach, there is an emphasis on "academic areas with facts, ideas, skills" and that it is "based on research." In the opposite column outlining progressive ideas on curriculum, it states that progressive education is "often based on unproven theories." The same source suggests that in mathematics, traditionalists are said to believe in "direct instruction of math concepts" which utilize "drill and skill." On the other hand, the author charges that progressives favor "interactive and discovery learning" or what is called "fuzzy math," which rejects memorization. A third example of a somewhat slanted comparison is found in the category called character development, where the progressives are said to believe in "relativism," while the traditionalists are committed to the goals of "citizenship" and "self-control."[3]

Needless to say, the progressives have been guilty of writing their own comparisons that favor their point of view. An illustration of such an approach would be a list of contrasts prepared by Helen Heyl, a former supervisor of the University of the State of New York, who published the following comparisons in an article of the *Journal of Education* in 1932. She wrote that in the traditional school, a child is sent to school and "kept until four o' clock, after which he explodes into freedom!" She writes about the progressive school that the "child goes to school and cannot get there early enough, he lingers in shops, lavatories, yards, and libraries until dusk or urgent parents drag him homeward." In contrasting what students do in school, she suggests that the traditional school students listen and the progressive school students work. A final example would be her belief that in a traditional school, a "child's mind is submitted to the grindstone of an educational discipline which dwarfs his capacity to think for himself." For her, the children who are lucky enough to attend a progressive school are "taught to think, to develop tolerant understanding, to question critically, and to evaluate."[4]

A twenty-first-century comparison that is perhaps somewhat more neutral is shown below.

Table 1

Traditional Approach	Progressive Approach
The specific curriculum and educational outcomes as well as the majority of the classes to be taken are prescribed by the state or local district.	The currculum is more flexible and is influenced by student interest.
Teachers have as their primary function introducing students to content knowledge and skills as outlined in the mandated curriculum.	Teachers are facilitators of learning who provide a learning environment in which students can use a wide variation of activities to learn in large part through discovery
The tools used by teachers are primarily textbooks and workbooks. Today these are being supplemented often by the use of technology such as powerpoint presentations.	Progessive teachers use a wider variety of materials and activities which allow individual and group research. This often includes the utilization of community resources.

In attempting to define the view of progressive educators, perhaps the single most important document can be found in a publication of the Progressive Education Association in 1918. Among the principles included in this historic document were the following.

I. *Freedom to develop naturally*

The conduct of the people should be governed by himself according to the social needs of his community, rather than by arbitrary laws. Full opportunity for initiative and self-expression should be provided.

II. *Interest, the motive of all work*

Interest should be satisfied and developed through: (1) direct and indirect contact with the world and its activities, and the use of the experiences thus gained; (2) application of knowledge gained, and correlation between different subjects; (3) the consciousness of achievement.

III. *The teacher a guide, not a taskmaster*

Progressive teachers will encourage the use of all the senses, training the pupils in both observation and judgment, and, instead of hearing recitations only, will spend most of the time teaching how to use various sources of information, including life activities as well as books, how to reason about the information thus acquired, and how to express forcefully and logically the conclusions reached.

IV. *Scientific study of pupil development*

School records should not be confined to the marks given by the teachers to show the advancement of the pupils in the study of a subject, but should also include both objective and subjective reports on those physical, mental, moral, and social characteristics which affect both school and adult life and which can be influenced by the school and the home. Such records should be used as a guide for the treatment of each pupil.

V. *The Progressive School a leader in educational movements*

The Progressive School . . . should be a laboratory where new ideas, if worthy, meet encouragement; where tradition alone does not rule but the best of the past is leavened with the discoveries of today, and the result is freely added to the sum of educational knowledge.[5]

Even given the difficulties involved in pinpointing the differences between traditionalists and progressives, one cannot deny the fact that the competition between these two camps has been a prominent theme in the history of education in the United States, beginning even before the twentieth century. In alluding to this ongoing struggle, David J. Ferrero has written in an article published in *Educational Leadership* that:

In fact, education's fiercest and most intractable conflicts have stemmed from differences in philosophy. Take the 100 Years' War between "progressives" and "traditionalists." To oversimplify an already oversimplified dichotomy, progressives incline toward pedagogical approaches that start with student interest and emphasize hands-on engagement with the physical and social environments, whereas traditionalists tend to start with pre-existing canons of inquiry and knowledge and emphasize ideas and concepts mediated through words and symbols.[6]

The purpose of this book is to first trace the events in what Ferrero labels "the 100 Years' War." Such an effort will include discussions about the origin of the progressive education movement as well as considering how the ideas of the progressives have influenced education during the various eras of the twentieth century. In choosing the title *The Progressive Education: Is It Still a Factor in Today's Schools?* I have hypothesized that certain events, especially during the past quarter century, may result in the final decline in this country of the progressive ideas and methods which emerged in the beginning of the twentieth century. The trends include the "back to basics" movement, curriculum standards, high-stakes testing, and accountability, which have resulted in part from the *A Nation at Risk* report and other studies made during the 1980s. There is no question that these documents have influenced the direction of education. Perhaps even more important is the passage of the No Child Left Behind legislation in 2002. It would seem that the traditionalists are very much in control during this first decade of the twenty-first century and those today who are willing to admit that they are either liberals in politics or progressive educators seem to be an endangered species. Even as I begin this project, I am less and less certain that given the waxing and waning of the theories of progressive education in the past, that to refer to the "fall" of progressive education might not be accurate. With that caution in mind, let us begin our journey through the progressive education movement.

NOTES

1. Ben Brodinksy, "Top 10 Education Events of the 20th Century," *Education Digest*, 64, no. 8, April 1999, 4–7.
2. Diane Ravitch, *Left Back: A Century of Battles Over School Reform*, (New York: Touchstone, 2000), 54.
3. "The Ongoing 'Education Wars,'" *CEO* at www.ceopa.org/Education-Wars.html (accessed 8 July 2005), 3.
4. David Tyack, Robert Lowe, and Elisabeth Hansot, *Public Schools in Hard Times*, (Cambridge, MA: Harvard University Press, 1984), 151.
5. Allan C. Ornstein, *Teaching and Schooling in America*, (Boston: Pearson Education Group, Inc., 2003), 315.
6. David J. Ferrero, "Pathways to Reform: Start with Values," *Educational Leadership* 62, no. 5 (February 2005): 10.

1

The Rise of Progressive Education

The ideas associated with the progressive education movement did not suddenly emerge. In every historic era there have been individuals who have thought of teaching and learning in ways other than that which were accepted in the conventional wisdom of their time. One could write a book just about people who supported alternative ways of teaching. Perhaps the first well-known individual who evolved his own style was Socrates. As reported by his star pupil, Plato, Socrates did not even think of himself as a teacher. He believed that true understanding was developed in a pupil by using a question method that allowed students to find their own truth. Using this method, "the teacher persuades the student to think by questioning him about his beliefs, by setting before him other beliefs and forcing him to probe the workings of his mind. In this way, the student accepts the truth, but only because it is true for him."[1] There are many other examples of individuals who have sought alternative ways to teach. Jesus relied heavily on the use of memorable parables to help his listeners to understand his lessons.

For the purpose of this project, it would be helpful to consider the individuals who most affected the thinking of the leaders of the American progressive education movement. A person who greatly impacted our nation's political beliefs was also interested in education. John Locke was an Englishman who lived primarily in the seventeenth century whose thoughts about government and democracy significantly affected the thinking of Thomas Jefferson and other leaders of the American Revolution. In the field of education, Locke believed that "truth and knowledge . . . arise out of observation and experience rather than from manipulation of accepted or given ideas."[2] Locke was thinking about education during his lifetime in a way that was adopted by the progressive educational leaders. Both Locke and these leaders believed that it was the role of the schools and of teachers to do more than pass on knowledge to their students. Locke was perhaps one of the first to suggest that concrete experiences were needed if students were to truly learn. Beyond this, he clearly saw that these experiences should be tailored to the individual needs and capacities of students. In this regard, he was extremely sensitive to the "innate differences between individuals." He wrote about the level of "energy, practice, and repetition children happily put into play, and therefore suggested dice and play-things with letters on them to teach children the alphabet."[3] This too was a foreshadowing of progressive thinking.

Perhaps even of greater influence than Locke was the work of French philosopher Jean-Jacques Rousseau. In his famous book, *Emile*, published first in 1762, he argues against an education based on subordination to a teacher and memorization. Rousseau claims that students learn best when they have concrete experiences and discover truth for themselves. Because he believed that children are born inherently "good," he was supportive of allowing more freedom and a "more permissive form of instruction."[4] He went so far as to suggest that "book knowledge would only corrupt children."[5] Rousseau's views certainly affected the thinking of American educators, including both Horace Mann and John Dewey.[6]

Another European, Johann Heinrich Pestalozzi (1746–1827), had beliefs similar to Rousseau. This closeness is symbolized by the fact that he kept a copy of *Emile* by his bedside throughout his adult life. Pestalozzi complemented Rousseau's thinking by using the emerging social science of psychology to further the idea of developing a new way to educate children. Although he did not consider himself an educator and wrote very little about teaching and learning, Pestalozzi is described by some as the "father of modern educational science." In a system called "object teaching" he advocated "inducing learning through direct experience with objects." Along with Herbart and Frobel, his work was instrumental in the establishment of the early progressive schools in America by Francis W. Parker and John Dewey.[7] Pestalozzi believed that "the natural instincts of the

child should provide the motives for learning rather than external prod-
ding and compulsion . . . the teacher's task is one of adapting instruction
to the individual child accordingly as his nature unfolds in the various
stages of natural development."[8]

Leaving the European forebears of the progressive education movement, we turn now to the events and personalities in the United States that
have influenced the movement. It should be noted that the first schools in
colonial America would be characterized as being extremely traditional.
The teacher's task was to tell and to drill. Discipline was often extremely
harsh and corporal punishment was the primary method for maintaining
discipline. Children were asked to memorize large sections of a limited
number of books that often included the Bible. The young men whose parents could afford the tuition to the private secondary schools would be expected to learn Greek and Latin by rote. It was to this practice that one of
our earliest educational innovators reacted. Early in his career, Benjamin
Franklin wrote a plan for a school in Philadelphia that would bear his
name. He wanted to establish a school that emphasized English rather
than Latin. The curriculum would tend toward practical subjects designed
to prepare children for careers in business and professions other than the
clergy.[9]

The notion of schools giving students a "useful" education was one that
resonated with many progressive educators. Franklin has written that, "it
would be well if [students] could be taught every Thing that is useful,
every Thing that is ornamental: But Art is long, and their Time is short. It
is therefore Propos'd that they learn Things that are likely to be most useful and most ornamental."[10] The Franklin Academy, which was established in 1751, offered classes in mathematics, astronomy, athletics, nav-
igation, dramatics, and bookkeeping. Students had some choice as to what
they would learn. In addition, the school accepted both boys and girls and
would become a model for the six thousand private academies founded in
the nineteenth century. These institutions, which required that most parents pay tuition, were the forerunners of the public high schools, which
evolved at the end of the century.[11]

The father of the public school movement in the United States, Horace
Mann, was in many ways a traditional educator, but for the time in which
he lived, in the middle of the nineteenth century, he had some rather progressive ideas. For instance, Mann believed that positive experiences

were the best motivation for learning. In his second report to the Board of Education of Massachusetts, he wrote that:

> Children, who spend six months in learning the alphabet, will, on the playground in a single half day or moonlight evening, learn the intricacies of a game or sport—where to stand, when to run, what to say, how to count, and what are the laws and the ethics of the game; —the whole requiring more intellectual effort that would suffice to learn half a dozen alphabets . . . the process of learning words and letters is toilsome and progress will be slow, unless a motive is inspired before instruction is attempted.[12]

In the same document, he suggested that teachers must have:

> Knowledge of methods and processes. These are indefinitely various . . . he who is apt to teach is acquainted, not only with common methods for common minds but with peculiar methods for pupils of peculiar dispositions and temperaments; and he is acquainted with the principles of all methods, whereby he can vary his plan, according to any differences of circumstances.[13]

Another indication of Mann's views on teaching can be learned by the instructional method he would use late in his life as a teacher at Antioch College. A former pupil, Henry Clay Badger, kept a diary during his years as a student at Antioch. He wrote that Mann would assign "special lessons" to individual students, giving each "some question to pursue at leisure and upon which to prepare a paper to be read to the whole class."[14] For this student, at least, what was exciting about Mann's teaching was "the impetus with which his mind smote our minds." He "kindled a heat of enthusiasm."[15] Undoubtedly this important educational pioneer demonstrated in his own teaching that the instructor's role was more than passing on information to his students. The fact is that he, like the progressives, believed that "rote learning of names and rules was neither effective nor desirable."[16]

Along with Mann, there were others who reacted against traditional teaching during his lifetime. Experimental schools could be found in isolated areas even during the nineteenth century, but as a nation, the major movement to change schools did not emerge until the last decade of the 1800s. It would truly gather momentum as a part of what historians have called the Progressive Movement at the beginning of the twentieth century.

In his book *The Good Years*, Walter Lord describes the sense of optimism that could be found in the United States as the nation began the twentieth century. He entitled his book "The Good Years" because "whatever the trouble, people were sure they could fix it." A *New York Times* editorial published on December 31, 1899, claimed that "we step upon the threshold of 1900 which leads to a new century, . . . facing a still brighter dawn of civilization." From their pulpits, clergy also were extremely positive about the new century. One clergy was quoted in the newspaper as saying that the "laws are becoming more just, values more humane; music is becoming sweeter and books wiser."[17]

The progressive education movement can be seen as part of a larger movement dominated by white middle-class Americans. The entire era beginning in 1901 until our entrance into World War I in 1917 has been labeled the progressive period. For many historians, this era of reform began when Theodore Roosevelt ascended to the presidency after the assassination of William McKinley. The reform causes that were part of the movement were varied and included such efforts as the regulation of big business, governmental reform, women's suffrage, and temperance. The progressives were not revolutionaries, but rather people who were interested in fixing specific problems and improving upon the status quo. Many individuals who might have been conservatives at other times were actively engaged in changing the system.

Stimulated by a group of writers who have been labeled "muckrakers" and led by progressive presidents including Theodore Roosevelt and Woodrow Wilson, laws were passed on the state and federal level that were meant to bring about progress in solving specific problems. Businesses were regulated by such legislation as the Meat Inspection Act, the Pure Food and Drug Act, and the Clayton Antitrust Law. A number of western states began the movement toward women's suffrage that would be completed with the passage of the Nineteenth Amendment in 1920. New democratic initiatives, such as recall votes and referendums, were introduced in a number of states. Progress was also made in regulating child labor and working conditions for adults.

Throughout the United States, attitudes shifted and the laissez-faire philosophy that dominated national life throughout the nineteenth century seemed to be eclipsed by an openness to change. The stirrings of change were present in the 1890s as writers pointed out defects in our system, and many of these issues emerged because we had moved from being a primarily agricultural nation to one that was becoming increasingly industrial. The Populist movement during the nineteenth century, even though it occurred mainly in rural areas, did raise issues that middle-class Americans in the urban and suburban communities felt should be addressed. Because of the widespread support of the more affluent and influential citizens, progressives were able to accomplish goals that were impossible for the Populists. It is also true that the reforms that occurred during the period before World War I were not nearly as far-reaching as those proposed by the Populists. Some historians have argued that progressivism also had a conservative strain that kept change from being overly dramatic. For example, there was little support for opening the system for wider participation by racial minorities.[18]

In the field of education, intellectuals and middle-class professionals were open to reading the books of John Dewey and others, even if most people were not necessarily ready to radically alter the schools. While there have always been parents willing to entrust their children to experimental schools that utilize new teaching methods, the number of such families has always been small. Historians have not agreed on the reason for the openness to new educational theories during the years before World War I. "Cubberley's interpretation of the educational changes in the late nineteenth and early twentieth centuries was that education changed simply to solve social and economic problems. Within this framework, the school is seen as a mere captive to social conditions." Primarily what was happening was that the United States was changing from an agricultural society to one dominated by industry and big business. In a later study, historian Merle Curti "contends that the majority of educational changes that occurred at the time were designed to serve the interests of the owners of industrial enterprises. For instance, he argues that vocational education and manual training were attempts to control and counteract radicalism among American workers." Lawrence Cremin is more idealistic as he suggested that educational progressivism is truly "a many-sided effort to use the schools to improve the lives of individuals."[19]

Undoubtedly all of the forces that stimulated the larger progressive movement were also at work in the field of education. There were certainly conditions in our schools that were ripe for change. With few exceptions, the public school systems at the end of the century were very traditional. Most teachers considered their primary role to be as information givers. As in other fields, there was perhaps a need to alter education to better fit the realities of twentieth-century life. Whether or not this is true, there were enough Americans open to new ideas that the innovations suggested by progressive educators would be given serious consideration. To begin our study of the meaning and impact of progressive education, we now turn to the individual who is most closely associated with the movement.

NOTES

1. George F. Kneller, ed., *Foundations of Education*, (New York: John Wiley and Sons, Inc., 1967), 124.

2. R. Freeman Butts and Lawrence A. Cremin, *A History of Education in American Culture*, (New York: Henry Holt and Co., 1953), 55.

3. Richard Aldrich, "John Locke," *Prospects*, 24, no. 1/2 (1994): 61–76.

4. Joel Spring, *The American School: 1642–1990*, (New York: Longman, 1990), 132.

5. Frederick Mayer, *American Ideas and Education*, (Columbus: Charles E. Merrill Books, Inc., 1964), 154.

6. Mayer, *American Ideas and Education*, 155.

7. Butts and Cremin, *A History of Education in American Culture*, 437–38.

8. Butts and Cremin, *A History of Education in American Culture*, 380

9. Myra Pollack Sadker and David Miller Sadker, *Teachers, Schools, and Society, 6th Edition*, (Boston: McGraw-Hill, 2003), 310.

10. Spring, *The American School: 1642–1990*, 19–20.

11. Sadker and Sadker, *Teachers, Schools, and Society, 6th Edition*, 310.

12. Lawrence A. Cremin, *The Republic and the School*, (New York: Bureau of Publications, Teachers College, Columbia University, 1957), 38–39.

13. Motivational Quotes for Teachers," at http://www.pitt.edu/~poole/ARCHIVE#.HTML, (accessed 14 March 2005), 2.

14. Louise Hall Tharpe, *Until Victory: Horace Mann and Mary Peabody*, (Boston: Little, Brown and Company, 1953), 279–80.

15. Tharpe, *Until Victory: Horace Mann and Mary Peabody*, 279–80.

16. Robert Badolato, The Educational Theory of Horace Mann," at www.newfoundations.com/GALLERY/Mann.html, (accessed 27 September 2004), 2.

17. Walter Lord, *The Good Years*, (New York: Harper and Row Publishing, 1960), 213.

18. Foster Rhea Dullis, *The United States Since 1865*, (Ann Arbor: University of Michigan Press, 1971), 178–81.

19. Spring, *The American School: 1642–1985*, 152–53.

2

John Dewey

Both high school and college American history textbooks, as well as those written specifically on the field of education, have consistently named John Dewey as the most significant educational philosopher in the United States during the twentieth century. His accomplishments are included prominently with those who affected other causes during the progressive period. For example, a much-used college history textbook written by Samuel Eliot Morison and Henry Steele Commager calls Dewey "the nation's most distinguished philosopher."[1] Typical of the references to Dewey in high school textbooks would be a statement such as "under the leadership of Professor John Dewey, an effort was made to rid American schools of the rigid, factory-like atmosphere which had long prevailed."[2] A second example would be an excerpt from the high school text *The Making of Modern America*, which stated:

> A man whose philosophy of education greatly influenced the schools of our times was John Dewey, a professor of philosophy at Columbia University. Until the time of Dewey, the schools of this country had aimed at giving the pupils little except factual knowledge. Dewey argued that a school should be a place where the student learns about life by actually living it. Thus a school had to offer more than book learning. It must give the student contact with nature and community life. It must attempt to develop the child's personality.[3]

Born in 1859 in Burlington, Vermont, John Dewey was the third son of Civil War veteran and village grocer Archibald Sprague Dewey and Lucinda Artimisin Rich Dewey. Dewey's mother was twenty years younger than her husband and came from a "well respected and public spirited Vermont family." Her grandfather had represented Vermont in the House of Representatives, and she herself was extremely active in social reform efforts in the community. As a parent, she impressed upon the entire family the need to be responsible for others in their community. John's mother also made certain that the family was active in the Burlington First Congregational Church. Because of the influence of the church as well as their mother, the Dewey children learned it was their duty to be involved citizens. John also observed the working of the town meetings and became a strong supporter of democratic decision-making. Because he attended a school that allowed students to skip grades, he was able to learn at his own pace and completed his elementary education in only five years.[4]

Graduating from high school at the age of fifteen, he entered the nearby University of Vermont, where he was described as a "shy" and "introspective" student whose grades were merely "average." The curriculum at the college was the same for all students until their senior year, when they took a course "designed to introduce students to the world of ideas." This class had the effect of stimulating the thinking of Dewey. At the time of his graduation he had no firm plan for his future, and he ended up accepting a teaching position in Oil City, Pennsylvania. This job paid the "relatively high salary" of forty dollars a month. During his two years in Pennsylvania, Dewey found time to publish an article titled "The Metaphysical Assumptions of Materialism" in the *Journal of Speculative Philosophy*. Following these two years of teaching away from home, he returned to Vermont to take his second teaching position. Soon after, with the financial help of a family member, he entered the graduate program in philosophy at Johns Hopkins University.[5]

After completing his doctorate, Dewey took a college teaching position at the University of Michigan, where with the exception of a year at the University of Minnesota, he taught for a decade. At age thirty-five, the young philosophy professor moved to the newly established University of Chicago. Although he had already published two books, it was in Chicago that he had the opportunity to test some of the theories that he was beginning to write about. His founding of a laboratory school allowed him to work directly with teachers who were using a variety of teaching techniques in their classrooms. As a result, he was able to publish *The School and Society*, which was the first of his many books dealing with education.[6]

While in Chicago he also worked with the famous social reformer Jane Addams at her well-known Hull House. His work there and at the laboratory school were major factors in shaping his thinking about education. It was at this point in time that he articulated his philosophy in a publication entitled "My Pedagogic Creed." After a dispute concerning the administration of the laboratory school, Dewey left the University of Chicago to accept a position in New York City at Columbia University. It was here where he would continue for many years to be the most prominent national figure in the progressive education movement. His presence at Columbia would help to make the university "a magnet for educators around the world." In 1916 his publication of *Democracy in Education* further enhanced his reputation as the nation's foremost educational philosopher. Traveling to China in 1919 and again in 1921, Dewey began to spread his ideas outside of the United States. Later he would lecture in Turkey, Mexico, South Africa, and Russia as well. Officially retiring in 1930, he remained active at the university as an emeritus professor until 1939. Even in his eighties, Dewey was an active and influential figure in American education until his death in 1952.[7]

Reviewing the biography of John Dewey is a much simpler task than attempting to summarize his philosophy of education. To begin with, his writing spans six decades, and his ideas understandably do not remain stagnant over the course of his long and productive life. When reading a book or article written by John Dewey, it is helpful to attempt to place it in context with the educational debates at the time of its publication. Authors of textbooks too often have attempted to summarize his views by choosing one or two of his books to highlight. Such an approach fails to encompass the entirety of his philosophy and to account for the additions and modifications made over the years. Coupled with this difficulty is the problem of easily understanding his writing. Justice Oliver Wendell Holmes has been quoted saying "although Dewey's book is incredibly ill-written, it seemed to me after several rereadings to have a feeling of intimacy with the inside of the cosmos that I found unequaled. So methought God would have spoken had He been inarticulate but keenly desirous to tell how it was."[8]

Perhaps a good place to begin in attempting to summarize Dewey's views would be his own summary that was published first in 1897, when he was thirty-eight years old. In doing so, it must be emphasized that some of these ideas were modified during his lifetime. Appearing in the *School Journal*, the article outlines what the then-young professor believed about education. In defining education, he wrote in part that:

> I believe that all education proceeds by the participation of the individual in the social consciousness of the race. This process begins unconsciously almost at birth, and is continually shaping the individual's powers, saturating his consciousness, forming his habits, training his ideas, and arousing his feelings and emotions. . . . I believe that the only true education comes through the stimulation of the child's powers by the demands of the social situations in which he finds himself. . . . I believe that this educational process has two sides—one psychological and one sociological . . . of these two sides the psychological is the basis. The child's own instincts and powers furnish the material and give the starting point for all education . . . Without insight into the psychological structure and activities of the individual, the educative process will . . . be haphazard and arbitrary. . . . Education, therefore, must begin with a psychological insight into the child's capacities, interests, and habits.[9]

The second part of the article speaks to the question "what the school is." Dewey wrote that:

> I believe that education, therefore, is a process of living and not a preparation for future living. I believe that the school must represent present life-life as real and vital to the child as that which he carries on in the home, in the neighborhood, or on the playground.

He goes on later to criticize the current schools in the United States.

> I believe that much of the present education fails because it neglects this fundamental principle of the school as a form of community. . . . The teacher is not in school to impose certain ideas or to form certain habits in the child, but is there as a member of the community to select the influences which shall affect the child and to assist him in properly responding to these influences. . . . Examinations are of use only so far as they test the child's fitness for social life and reveal the place in which he can be of most service and where he can receive the most help.

In regard to the subject matter of education, he writes, "I believe, therefore, that the true center of correlation on the school subjects is not science, nor literature, nor history, nor geography, but the child's own social activities." This final idea is one that led some of his followers to dismiss totally the idea of an established curriculum and textbooks. Later in his life, Dewey would criticize those who tried to teach without establishing some sort of structure for student learning.

Finally, regarding teaching methods, he wrote that:

I believe that the question of method is ultimately reducible to the question of the order of development of the child's powers and interest. . . . I believe that much of the time and attention now given to the presentation of lessons might be more wisely and profitably expended in training the child's power of imagery and in seeing to it that he was continually forming definite, vivid, and glowing images of the various subjects with which he comes in contact in his experience.[10]

These ideas would be expanded upon and refined over the years. Other elements of this philosophy are included in the voluminous scholarship of this extremely prolific writer. One respected education historian, Joel Spring, has done a better job than many in summarizing Dewey's views. He too, speaks of the difficulty of such an effort, pointing out the "complexity" of Dewey's writing and the fact that it is often "open to varying interpretations." Several of Spring's observations are very helpful. For instance, he emphasizes Dewey's consistent conviction that children are not "primarily motivated to learn by rewards and punishment." For Dewey, he suggests, "the source of individual action is not stimulation from an outside reward or punishment, but originates in individual interests and desires.[11] This view leads to the notion that what happens in school should be based on student interests. Spring gives the following example:

A student or students might express an interest in milk. The teacher would guide the students to the sources of the production, chemistry, and distribution of milk. Groups of students might visit the local dairy and develop a group project on milk for the classroom. During this group study of milk, students might learn chemistry, economics, arithmetic, social history, and cooperation.[12]

Others have emphasized Dewey's conception of education as primarily "a social process."

His pragmatic theory of knowledge led him to look upon thinking as an educational method of problem solving. His whole philosophic and educational outlook was based upon a conception of experience that led him to affirm that education should be grounded firmly upon moral commitments to a democratic way of life.[13]

The best way to do this for Dewey was using the scientific method. He suggested that this included the following steps:

1. Defining the problem that is raised by some upset or difficulty or disturbance.
2. Observing the conditions surrounding the problem.
3. Formulating hypotheses that might solve the problem.
4. Elaboration of the possible consequences of acting upon several alternative hypotheses.
5. Active testing to see which alternative idea best solves the problem.[14]

In addition to discussing his evolving thoughts on education, some authors have highlighted that an equally important contribution was his effective criticism of schools during his lifetime. In his own words, Dewey described the schools of his day as follows.

The traditional scheme is, in essence, one of imposition from above and from outside. It imposes adult standards, subject matter, and methods upon those who are only growing slowly toward maturity. The gap is so great that the required subject matter, the methods of learning and of behaving are foreign to the existing capacities of the young. They are beyond the reach of the experience the young learners already possess. Consequently, they must be imposed . . . learning here means acquisition of what already is incorporated in books and in the heads of the elders. Moreover, that which is taught is thought of as essentially static. It is taught as a finished product, with little regard either to the ways in which it was originally built up or to the changes that will surely occur in the future. It is to a large extent the cultural product of societies that assume the future would be much like the past, and yet it is used as education food in the society where change is the rule, not the exception.[15]

While Dewey was very effective in articulating the deficiencies of traditional education, his own ideas have spawned many critics. For those who disagree with his "child-centered" approach and "learning by doing," his philosophy fails to give enough attention to the need to transmit our cultural heritage and also does not acknowledge that children must often "apply effort" before they develop academic interests. Others are less than impressed with Dewey's affection for using the scientific method to solve every problem. They suggest that it is essential that children learn subjects "systematically, and not experimentally." For the critics, too many American students fail to master the required subject matter, especially in science and math. A number of other scholars have claimed that Dewey's philosophy and methods are "highly relativistic and situational" and that the approach does not allow for "the existence of universal truths and values."[16]

It also should be pointed out that although Dewey often suggested that teacher education students should be taught using the type of techniques that they would use later in their own classes, he himself, although an extremely effective lecturer, was the most traditional of teachers. One of his pupils, philosopher Erwin Edman, describes his experience in Dewey's graduate class as follows:

He sat at his desk, fumbling with a few crumpled yellow sheets and looking abstractly out of the window. He spoke very slowly in a Vermont drawl. He looked very kindly and very abstracted. He hardly seemed aware of the presence of a class. He took little pains to underline the phrase, or emphasize a point, or, so at first seemed to me, to make any. . . . He seemed to be saying whatever came into his head next. . . . The end of the hour finally came and he simply stopped; it seemed to me that he might have stopped anywhere. But I soon found that it was my mind that had wandered, not John Dewey's. I began very soon to do what I had seldom done in college courses—to take notes. It was then a remarkable discovery to make . . . to find that what had seemed so casual, so rambling, so unexciting, was of an extraordinary coherence, texture, and brilliance. I had been listening not to the semi-theatrical repetition of a discourse many times made—a fairly accurate description of many academic lectures—I had been listening to a man actually *thinking* in the presence of a class.[17]

Whether or not Dewey utilized in his classes the methods that he advocated for teachers in the public schools, there is little question that his ideas have become a significant factor in the educational debates that have been so much a part of our twentieth century. One of the problems facing anyone trying to analyze the impact of Dewey is his prolific output of forty books and some five hundred articles. Education textbooks have chosen just a few of these ideas to pass on to future generations of teachers and school administrators. For example, in the book *The History of American Education*, L. Dean Webb chose the following views of Dewey to emphasize:

- Dewey favored a curriculum based on the interests of the children to be taught as opposed to a strict subject matter curriculum developed by adults. Late in his career he criticized those who went too far in carrying out this goal. He came to believe that there needed to be some structure to the organization of classroom activities.
- Dewey was against rote memorization and favored "learning by doing," which was the model of his laboratory school at the University of Chicago. For him, classroom activities should be real-life experiences that were meaningful to the children at their stage of development.
- A primary goal of education should be to promote "individual growth" and to prepare children for full participation in a democratic society. Schools should be a miniature democratic institutions, which in his own words, would promote "a spirit of social cooperation and community life."
- Schools should do much more than deal with the intellectual development of students but also should be concerned with their social, emotional, and physical needs.[18]

Sadker and Sadker, in their popular educational textbook for students in teacher education, *Teachers, Schools, and Society*, highlight these views of Dewey:

- Dewey believed that education should teach students to be problem solvers in order to understand and control their environment. Classroom experiences should be designed to help students to solve problems.

- He strongly supported the use of the scientific method as the appropriate approach to solve these problems.[19]

A historical movement such as progressive education can seldom be attributed to the work of any one individual. Certainly in considering the changes in education during the twentieth century, there were a number of important contributors. In order to better understand the unfolding of the progressive education movement, it will be helpful now to consider several of the other leading figures.

NOTES

1. Samuel Eliot Morison and Henry Steele Commager. *The Growth of the American Republic*, (New York: Oxford University Press, 1960), 308.

2. Avery O. Craven. *American History*, (Boston: Ginn and Co., 1961), 584.

3. Leon H. Canfield and Howard B. Wilder. *The Making of Modern America*, (Boston: Houghton Mifflin Co., 1962), 599.

4. Gerald L. Gutek. *Historical and Philosophical Foundations of Education*. (Upper Saddle River, NJ: Pearson Prentice Hall, 2005), 337–38.

5. L. Glenn Smith and Joan K. Smith. *Lives in Education*, (New York: St. Martin's Press, 1994), 287.

6. "John Dewey (1859–1952)," James Phiser, PhD. http://www.iep.utm.edu/d/dewey.htm (accessed 8 July, 2005), 1–2.

7. "John Dewey," Jim Garrison, College of Human Resources and Education, Virginia Tech. http://www.vusst.hr/ENCYCLOPEDIA/john_dewey.htm (accessed 10 November 1999), 2–3.

8. Frank Fridel. *America in the 20th Century*, (New York: Alfred A Knopf, 1960), 145.

9. John Dewey. "My Pedagogic Creed," http://www.infed.org/archives/e-texts/e-dew-pc.htm (accessed 4 August, 2005) 1–2. 3–5.

10. Dewey, "My Pedagogic Creed," 7–9.

11. Joel Spring, *American Education*, (Boston: McGraw-Hill, 1998), 245.

12. Spring, *American Education*, 245.

13. R. Freeman Butts and Lawrence A. Cremin, *A History of Education in American Culture*, (New York: Henry Holt and Co., 1953), 344.

14. Butts and Cremin, *A History of Education in American Culture*, 346.

15. Newton Edwards and Herman G. Richey, *The School in the American Social Order*, (Boston: Houghton Mifflin Company, 1963), 543–43.

16. Allan C. Ornstein, *Teaching and Schooling in America*, (Boston: Pearson Education Group, Inc., 2003), 144.

17. Gilbert Highat, *The Art of Teaching*, (New York: Vintage Books, 1950), 211.

18. L. Dean Webb, *The History of American Education*, (Upper Saddle River, NJ: Pearson Prentice Hall, 2006), 144.

19. Myra Pollack Sadker and David Miller Sadker, *Teachers, Schools, and Society, 7th Edition*, (Boston: McGraw-Hill, 2005), 314–15.

3

Other Pioneers in the Progressive Education Movement

Despite a tendency of the authors of general American history books to associate progressive education with John Dewey, there are a number of his contemporaries who were also very instrumental in affecting how teachers taught and how learning would take place in our classrooms during the twentieth century. Choosing which of these educational leaders to highlight in this brief account is a daunting task. Perhaps the place to begin is with a brief discussion about the man whom Dewey referred to in a 1930 issue of *The New Republic*, in which he wrote that Colonel Francis Parker "more than any one person, was the father of the progressive educational movement."[1]

With very little formal education, Francis Parker began his teaching career at age sixteen.[2] Two years later in 1861, he helped to raise a company of young men from his hometown in Manchester, New Hampshire. The group elected him as their lieutenant before they set off to go to war. During his distinguished military career, he led not only his hometown troops, but also newly enlisted Negro soldiers. After being shot in the neck, an injury that would affect his speaking voice for the rest of his life, he was commissioned as a lieutenant colonel. Later in the war, he was captured by the Confederate army. His experiences in the war caused him to be an acknowledged war hero, and he retained the title of colonel for the rest of his life. Upon returning home after the war, Parker spent several more years in New Hampshire until 1868, when he accepted a position with the

Dayton Ohio School District. When his wife died four years later, he chose
to become a student in Germany for the next two and a half years at the University of Berlin. It was here that he developed his interest in "the scientific
approach to lesson planning." After coming back to the United States in
1875, he became the Superintendent of Schools in Quincy, Massachusetts,
where he helped to develop his new ideas into a plan that was soon called
the "Quincy System." He left Massachusetts in 1883 to become the principal of a teacher-training institution in Chicago know as the Cook County
Normal School.[3] More than twenty years before Dewey's important book,
Democracy in Education, Parker wrote a best seller, *Talks on Pedagogics*,
which discusses a theme that was similar to Dewey's later classic. By then
he was convinced that it was "education not economics" that divided classes
and caused exploitation and alienation. Like Horace Mann and John Dewey,
Parker believed that "knowledge was power." Very conscious of significant
differences between the social classes in America, he opposed the idea that
upper-class children should be given a different education than that which
was available to the less well-off students. In 1894, he wrote that, "there is
no reason why one child should study Latin and another be limited to the
three R's."[4] In addition, Parker was also ahead of his time by calling for
racial integration in the public schools.

A frequent speaker at gatherings of educators, during the 1890s he became a missionary of progressive education ideas. Organizational changes
in Chicago caused some conflict between Francis Parker and John Dewey.
When Parker died suddenly in 1902, Dewey succeeded him at the University of Chicago as the Director of the School of Education. Very soon
afterwards a "full-scale war" developed between John Dewey and some
of Parker's supporters. This academic struggle was certainly one of the
reasons that Dewey left Chicago and accepted a position at Columbia,
where he would spend the rest of his career. As for Francis Parker, although his published works have been largely forgotten, his influence on
the early progressive education movement was undeniable.[5] Considering
Parker's career and writings in the field of education, one might summarize his thinking by listing the following themes. He preached that schools
must have a high regard and respect for the creative activity of the child.
With this in mind, he experimented with many kinds of school programs
such as the "core curriculum" that attempted to relate subjects of the curriculum through such interrelated studies as history and geography.[6] His

work in this area provided a starting point for John Dewey and later progressives. This approach was perhaps instrumental in the decision of educators in the twentieth century to combine history with the social sciences to create the new curriculum area known as social studies. Even as a teacher, early in his career, he assigned projects that required students to integrate math with other subjects. Vehemently opposed to rote learning, he believed that there was little value in knowing something that you don't understand. Because he was convinced that children were naturally active and curious, he also questioned the value of punishment and rewards as motivators. He even went so far as to question the value of assigning grades to students.[7] Like others who came later in the movement, Parker wrote that "the centre of all movement in education . . . is the child." This emphasis for him led to the undoubted need to carry on a scientific study of children.[8] Parker's growing concern for the differences in children led to a concept that is very much in vogue today. Called "differentiation," he experimented in the Quincy school district with slightly different programs for children of different abilities.[9] He also stressed "experience-based learning activities such as nature studies and field trips."[10]

Unlike Dewey and many of the other leaders of the movement, Parker's writing was based in part on years of direct experience as a teacher and school administrator. As an administrator, his schools went far beyond what many less adventuresome progressives were willing to attempt. Diane Ravitch, in her book *Left Back*, reports that Parker "eliminated not only the set curriculum but spellers, readers, and grammar textbooks; children learned words and sentences, not the alphabet."[11] In this way he was ahead of other progressives, as he was actually experimenting with what in the late twentieth century we have called "whole language." Although there were no standardized tests to validate Parker's methods, when the Massachusetts School Board visited Quincy, they concluded that "Quincy's youngsters actually stood ahead of the majority of Massachusetts school children."[12] Before anyone had ever heard the name of John Dewey, Francis Parker was widely known for his experimentation in the field of education. Despite his distinguished career, he will probably never have his name listed in a prominent place in American history textbooks, where his admirer John Dewey continues to reign supreme.

Still another individual who greatly influenced the development of progressive education was the Swiss psychologist Jean Piaget (1896–1980).

A well-known contemporary author in the field of education has written in his book, *The Schools Our Children Deserve*, that "in the case of progressive education, it can be safely said that two twentieth-century individuals, John Dewey and Jean Piaget, have shaped the way we think of this movement." Kohn writes that Piaget "demonstrated the way children think is qualitatively different from the way adults think and argues that a child's way of thinking progresses through a series of distinct stages."[13] Given these stages, Piaget and his associates sought to determine how children at each stage learn best. In doing so, they concluded that at any of the stages, "little learning is retained when it is learned on command." Like others in the progressive movement, he believed that students learn best when they were actively involved.[14]

In their book, *The History of Education in America*, John D. Pulliam and James J. Van Patten have written that:

> Piaget believed that the two fundamental characteristics of children's learning and cognitive development are organization and adaptation. Organization is described as the systematizing of information into meaningful patterns. These patterns are used to structure new information so that it does not seem random or chaotic to the learner. Adaptation is the process of coping, or integrating new information into existing perceptions and patterns. Intelligence for Piaget must follow from our ability to organize and adapt. Like Dewey, Piaget saw human beings as born active, curious, interested in communication, and with a need to assimilate information.[15]

Contemporary educators have utilized Piaget's theories in developing the teaching method known as "inquiry based instruction."[16] Other historians associate the psychological views of Piaget with the modern theory known as "constructivism." Whether it is called constructivism or progressivism, the premise is that "students would be motivated to learn only if they were active learners, constructing their own knowledge through their own discoveries."[17]

Although Piaget was never a teacher and "always refused the title educationist," his historic impact has come from the fact that so many progressive educators have referenced his work "to justify their methods and principles." Like Dewey, his writings are voluminous and were open at times to varying interpretations. A brilliant young man, he published articles in prestigious scientific journals at age fifteen. He, like other progressives, became convinced that, "the scientific approach was the only way of gaining access to human knowledge. . . . His attitude and his involvement in the field of education led him quite naturally to champion the pupil's active participation as the royal road to the scientific approach in school."[18]

With the other leaders of the progressive education movement, Piaget believed in the "active participation" of children in learning and felt strongly that "coercion is the worst of teaching methods." He wished to see schools "without coercion" where "pupils actively experience with a view to reconstructing for themselves what is learned." For him, like for Parker, "the ideal school would not have compulsory textbooks," but "reference books, which would be 'used freely.'"[19] He was certain that these reference books would be eagerly used by students if the topics being studied were appropriate to their developmental level and effectively introduced by a creative teacher.

In reaching this conclusion, he was very much in agreement with the other pioneers of the progressive movement. One of those individuals, who would become perhaps the most effective missionary in spreading the progressive education theories of Piaget and Dewey, was Professor William Heard Kilpatrick (1871–1965).

Kilpatrick was a favorite pupil of John Dewey. Dewey once described young Kilpatrick as "the best I have ever had."[20] Although he first had trouble understanding Dewey while taking classes at the University of Chicago, Kilpatrick became a champion of his professor after he had moved to Columbia. Prior to attending Columbia, he studied at Johns Hopkins University, but once he moved to New York, he remained there for the duration of his long career. Of his experience at Columbia as a student, he would say, "the work under Dewey remade my philosophy of life and education." He also was quoted as saying that "next after Plato and Aristotle and above Kant and Hegel," Dewey contributed most to "thought and life."[21]

Even if Dewey was an essential mentor to Kilpatrick, there is little question that Kilpatrick was important in his own right. It has been suggested that he would become "the most influential" progressive educator because of his ability to explain not only his own ideas, but those of others. Following his formal education, Kilpatrick took a position at his alma mater, Mercer College in Georgia. There he rose to the position of acting president before he

joined the faculty at Columbia University in 1909. He would have a distinguished career at Columbia until his retirement in 1938. Like Dewey, after
his retirement, he continued to be active as a writer and lecturer.[22]

Both as a lecturer and a college instructor, Kilpatrick excelled. Students
flocked to his classes in large numbers, and it was estimated that he taught
close to thirty-five thousand students during his long career. At Columbia,
he was known as "the million-dollar professor" because of the tuition
money that the university earned from his classes. Along with writing and
speaking about his own ideas on education, he became especially proficient in explaining the ideas of John Dewey. In his diary, Kilpatrick once
wrote, "I feel to some measure that I am best qualified of those about here
(Columbia) to interpret Dewey. His own lectures are frequently impene-
trable to even intelligent students."[23]

Personally Kilpatrick is best known for his project method of teaching.
The essential aspect of this technique was what he called a "socially pur-
poseful act." By this he meant that students were to be engaged in "an activity directed toward a socially useful end." This group learning process
was first introduced in a widely read article he wrote in 1918.[24] Like the
other pioneers in progressive education, Kilpatrick believed that students
should be active in their learning and that merely reading a book was most
often ineffective. Such learning he believed "tends to produce students
who at the close of a course, decisively shut the book and say, 'Thank gra-
cious, I am through with that!' How many people 'get an education,' and
yet hate books and hate to think?"[25] In contrast to this, author Alfie Kohn
quotes a modern-day progressive educator who describes a contemporary
class engaged in a version of Kilpatrick's project method. Such a classroom is described by the author in this way:

Walk into our classroom during project time, and you might see children
sprawled on the rug taking notes from books on the habitats of beavers or
on medieval life, or two students across the room watching a videotape on
Jane Goodall, or others conducting tests on the aerodynamics of paper air-
planes. Go to the library down the hall (past students rehearsing a play they
have written), and you might find members of the other half of the class
conducting research on virtual reality or the history of Halloween. If you
then go the computer lab, you'll see, for example, one student inputting survey data while another learns to write a new computer language. In short,
you never know what you might experience next, or, most important, what

the students might experience next. . . . Discipline problems are minimal because students are interested in what they are doing—they see their pursuits as having *purpose*.[26]

The project method was just one of the contributions of this man who was, according to one admirer, "the most popular professor in Teacher College history."[27] As a teacher, he was offering his students viable alternatives to the traditional teaching methods that Kilpatrick saw as emphasizing "efficiency, standardization, control, and manipulation." What he was talking about was an education that would unify "learning and living." In doing so, he was attempting to alter what had been happening in classrooms throughout the world for centuries. Students in the classrooms envisioned by Kilpatrick and Dewey would be alive with the democratic spirit. Democracy for Kilpatrick was "a way of life, a kind and quality of associated living in which sensitive moral principles assert the right to control individual and group conduct." His conception of democracy included more than a way to make political choices; it was "the way we live with each other, the way we treat one another in our daily interactions and relationships."[28] This goal of a democratic classroom environment might be similar to what modern educators are now seeking when they speak and write of the classroom as a "community of learners." It would provide a different classroom climate than the traditional environment where the teacher is primarily an information giver and disciplinarian.

In limiting this discussion to the contributions of Dewey, Parker, Piaget, and Kilpatrick, this account is unfair to many other individuals who have been significant contributors to the progressive education movement. To do justice to all of the pioneers in the movement would require several volumes. That is not the primary purpose of this book, so we must now move on to trace progressivism in education during the first half of the twentieth century.

NOTES

1. "Experiencing Education, Chapter One—Dewey Creates a New Kind of School." http://www.ucls.uchicago.edu/about/history/ee/chapter1_3.pdf (accessed 15 September 2005), 7.

2. Frederick Mayer, *American Ideas and Education*, (Columbus, OH: Charles E. Merrill Books, Inc. 1964), 309.

3. L. Glenn Smith and Joan K. Smith. *Lives in Education*, (New York: St. Martin's Press, 1994), 280–81.

4. Joel Spring, *The American School: 1642–1990*, (New York: Longman, 1990), 200.

5. Spring, *The American School: 1642–1990*, 282–288.

6. John D. Pulliam and James J. Van Patten, *The History of Education in America*, (Upper Saddle River, NJ: Merrill, 1991), 139.

7. Sanderson Beck, "Francis W. Parker's Concentration Pedagogy: Education to Free the Human Spirit," at www.san.beck.org/Parker.html (accessed 12 July 2005), 1–4.

8. R. Freeman Butts and Lawrence A. Cremin, *A History of Education in American Culture*, (New York: Henry Holt and Co., 1953), 383.

9. Butts and Cremin, *A History of Education in American Culture*, 429.

10. Gerald L. Gutek. *Historical and Philosophical Foundations of Education*. (Upper Saddle River, NJ: Pearson Prentice Hall, 2005), 356–57.

11. Diane Ravitch, *Left Back: A Century of Battles Over School Reform*, (New York: Touchstone, 2000), 357.

12. Butts and Cremin, *A History of Education in American Culture*, 438.

13. Alfie Kohn, *The Schools Our Children Deserve*, (Boston: Houghton Mifflin Co., 1999), 4–5.

14. Kohn, *The Schools Our Children Deserve*, 66.

15. Pulliam and Van Patten, *History of Education in America*, 172–73.

16. Pulliam and Van Patten, *History of Education in America*, 187.

17. Ravitch, *Left Back: A Century of Battles Over School Reform*, 441.

18. Alberto Munari, "Jean Piaget," *Prospects: The Quarterly Review of Comparative Education*, 34, no. ½, 1994, p. 311–327.

19. Munari, "Jean Piaget," 311–327.

20. "Child-Centered Wing, 1890–1930," at http://asterix.ednet.lsu.eu/~maxcy/4001_8.htm (accessed 14 June 2005), 7.

21. Landon E. Beyer, "William Heard Kilpatrick," *Prospects: The Quarterly Review of Comparative Education*, 27, no. 3, September 1997, 470–85.

22. Mayer, *American Ideas and Education*, 407.

23. Ravitch, *Left Back: A Century of Battles Over School Reform*, 178.

24. Spring, *The American School: 1642–1990*, 179.

25. Kohn, *The Schools Our Children Deserve*, 148.

26. Kohn, *The Schools Our Children Deserve*, 147.

27. Beyer, "William Heard Kilpatrick," *Prospects: The Quarterly Review of Comparative Education*, 9.

28. Beyer, "William Heard Kilpatrick," *Prospects: The Quarterly Review of Comparative Education*, 11.

4

The Progressive Education Movement during the First Half of the Twentieth Century

At the outset it must be acknowledged that like other aspects of our society, education has gone through "pendulum-like swings, from left to right and back again." Even accepting this phenomenon, there are observers who would claim that during the past hundred years, the way we have educated children in our mainstream schools has remained quite constant. The teaching approaches advocated by progressives have been utilized in every decade of the twentieth century, but they were most often confined primarily to a limited group of experimental schools. Many times, the progressive ideas would be tried in private schools as opposed to public schools. Looking back on a half century of work, John Dewey acknowledged that a majority of the changes that occurred in most schools were "atmospheric." At midcentury, he believed that progressive education had not "really penetrated and permeated the foundations of the educational institution."[1]

Others would disagree with Dewey's pessimistic assessment of the impact of progressive education. Historian Joel Spring points to the Social Education Association formed in 1906 by Colin Scott. The association's charter stated that "the fundamental purpose of education should be to prepare the child for a useful life of social service as an active and creative member of the social organism." Spring goes on to claim that because of this organization and the increasing exposure of readers to the works of John Dewey and others, the idea of "socialized classroom activity became popular." Books and articles on this new way of thinking were published in large numbers during the first two decades of the century.[2]

It was not only professional educators who were calling for changes in schools. Progressives in fields other than education also highlighted in their writing and in their work the importance of education. Jacob Riis, one of the most influential of the so-called muckrakers, raised this question in his best-selling book, *How the Other Half Lives*, "Do you see how the whole battle with the slum is fought out in and around the public school?" If we can reform schools "the battle with the slum will be over." The famous Chicago social worker, Jane Addams, the founder of Hull House, also supported changes in schools. A friend of John Dewey, she pointed out that:

> We are impatient with the schools which lay all stress on reading and writing, suspecting them to rest on the assumption that all knowledge and interest must be brought to the children through the medium of books. Such an assumption fails to give the child any clew to the life about him, or any power to usefully or intelligently connect himself with it.[3]

From 1902 until 1955 the Progressive Education Association, a group that included in its membership most of the prominent leaders of the movement, was active in promoting the need to develop a more student-centered approach to education. The organization "reached its peak of membership during the depression" when, with a grant, it conducted its "noted Eight-Year Study."[4] Although it has been criticized for the sampling of schools that it studied, author Alfie Kohn has written that "the Eight-Year Study, ought to have made far more of an impact than it did — and ought to be a lot better known than it is. It has quite rightly been called the best-kept educational secret of the twentieth century." Kohn described the study as follows:

> More than fifteen hundred students over four years were compared to an equal number of carefully matched students at conventional schools. The result: when they got to college, the experimental students did just as well as, and often better than, their traditionally educated counterparts on all counts: grades, extracurricular participation, and drop-out rate as well as on measures of such things as intellectual curiosity and resourcefulness. And here's the kicker: "the further a school departed from the traditional college preparatory program, the better was the record of its graduates."[5]

Despite the apparent success of the innovative methods of the progressive schools in the study, a researcher found at the end of the 1940s that most of the innovative teaching methods had been "short-lived" and that "there were few traces of the experimental programs left."[6]

However, one cannot discount the fact that in public and private schools all over the country, there were experiments taking place utilizing the theories of progressive educational philosophers. These experiments were taking place in all types of schools. For example, in the late 1930s, there were almost two hundred teachers in one-room schoolhouses in the state of Michigan who were using progressive methods that they had learned in in-service programs. California, perhaps more than any other state, tried to coordinate and stimulate the use of innovative teaching techniques from the state level. Using publications and state-sponsored conferences, the educational leaders attempted to spread the word. Reform efforts were made at both the elementary and the secondary level. Because state educational bureaucracies at the beginning of the century lacked the power that they have today, decisions on curriculum and teaching methods remained primarily a local prerogative. Whether a school district became heavily involved in the progressive education movement depended largely on the school district leaders. Districts that were geographical neighbors often varied greatly in their support of educational reform. Even within individual schools, teachers differed in their level of the interest and commitment to progressive goals and methods.[7]

One of the factors that affected the reform movement was the design of school buildings being used during the early twentieth century. Author Larry Cuban points out in his book *How Teachers Taught: Constancy and Change in American Classrooms, 1890–1980*, that "at the beginning of the century, the classrooms were constructed for forty and sixty students with bolted-down desks in rows facing the front of the rooms . . . in addition, teachers were poorly trained and often had to cover ten different subjects daily by using textbooks and curricula prescribed by the central administration."[8]

There was also a major trend at the beginning of the twentieth century to create schools in the industrial model of the times, which stressed organization and efficiency. Most large school districts used the corporation organizational pattern that emphasized a top-down management style. Under such a system, principals and teachers were expected to follow the orders of the newly empowered superintendents. Although some chief school officers and their boards of education were open to change, many were not.

One district that did seek to incorporate progressive methods was New York City. In 1934, the district introduced what was called the "activity program." The purpose of this plan was to allow "teachers and students working together to select subject matter and learning activities" while maintaining "a focus on the needs and interests of the students. In addition, classroom schedules were flexible, with the standard teacher-dominated recitation being replaced by excursions, research, dramatization, and sharing."

The system also eased up on classroom discipline methods and attempted to teach the students "self control."[9] Even though the experiment was short-lived, "observational data was highly favorable" when the activity-based schools were compared with more traditional programs. It appeared to the observers who did the research that the activity classes "showed more self-direction, initiative, participation, planning, experimentation, cooperation, leadership, and critical thinking without loss of discipline."[10]

Many other cities became embroiled in heated discussions over what should be taught in their high schools. Progressives charged that the academic curriculum that included the study of Latin and Greek for the college-bound students was elitist. Another aspect of the debate about high school curricula was whether academic subjects taught in the traditional manner truly helped to develop "mental discipline." The idea of the "mental discipline" concept was that if students learned to memorize Latin vocabulary, the process of learning this subject would carry over into learning other subjects. Progressives and liberal educators disagreed with "the alleged power gained from mental gymnastics."[11]

The progressives were helped in this debate by the work of psychologist Edward L. Thorndike, whose studies caused him to conclude "that school studies were effective only for specific, particular purposes, not for general improvement." Thus it appeared that memorizing or learning significant information in a history class would not necessarily create skills that would help in a math class. If this is indeed true, which it should be noted is not a conclusion accepted by all psychologists, one of the rationales for the traditional curriculum and teaching methods was greatly weakened. The lack of carryover from one academic subject to another was used by those progressives seeking to base curricula on "vocational concerns." Other progressives believed that the research helped their case for making curriculum decisions based on "children's immediate interests."[12]

This research helped to encourage such plans as the Dalton Laboratory Plan. In schools within Dalton, Massachusetts, the school day was divided into "subject labs." The approach, which is attributed to Helen Parkhurst, received national attention. Under the plan, students in grades five through twelve had no set schedules as the traditional classroom approach was abandoned. Because there were no bells, the students had much more control over their own learning. Teachers sought to use the students' individual interests as a guide to the curriculum.[13]

Another woman who was instrumental in implementing a progressive approach to education was Ella Flagg Young (1845–1917). As the first woman superintendent of a large city school district, she was also the first of her gender to be elected president of the National Education Association. After being his coworker in Chicago, Young would later receive credit from John Dewey for her support. He was quoted as saying "more times than I could say I didn't see the meaning or force of some favorite conception of my own until Mrs. Young had given it back to me. . . . It was from her that I learned that freedom and respect for freedom meant regard for the inquiring and reflective processes of individuals."[14] As they worked together at the famous Laboratory School in Chicago, both Mrs. Young and John Dewey concluded that "the school should mirror the democratic society it served." Unlike most administrators of her time, Young believed in participatory management and gave to both teachers and principals a significant role in decision-making. She was especially committed to having the principals be more than managers, as she wanted them to be instructional leaders in their building.[15]

Ella Flagg Young died in 1917, the year the United States entered World War I. Some historians have seen this war as a turning point in the progressive education movement. It has been argued that before the war, progressives were primarily concerned with the urban poor. The goal was to create opportunities for those whom society was leaving behind. Such innovations as vocational schools and health and nutrition programs were incorporated into the schools during the early years of the century.

According to L. Dean Webb, the change after the war was that the movement became more involved with:

> private schools or the public schools in suburbs serving middle- or upper-class families. The parents were not interested in the social services provided by the school or the vocational training it offered; they were impressed by the "new psychology" and the references to child-centeredness and creativity and wanted to see these ideas expanded in their schools.[16]

By the thirties it has been suggested that there was another shift in emphasis among progressives. The focus of the literature that was being produced by the leading educators dealt less with "student centered learning" and more with "the social and economic problems of the whole culture." "Many progressive educators continued with their experiments in natural development, the activity curriculum, and the child-centered school; however, the possibility of the schools as leaders in improving or reconstructing society became the theme of progressives like George Counts."[17]

Counts was the education spokesman for Franklin Delano Roosevelt's New Deal program. In a pamphlet titled *Dare the Schools Build a Social Order*, he argued that schools in the past had perpetuated economic and social classes. In doing so, our society had "neglected the interest of labor." His answer was "to reconstruct the school system." To do this, Counts wished to gain more representatives of labor on local school boards, expand vocational and adult education, and use the curriculum to "fight both social inequality and segregation." He strongly urged that schools become a force in the struggle to bring about social and economic reform.[18]

Whatever the specific focus of progressivism might have been during the first five decades of the twentieth century, these trends all impacted our educational system. For John Dewey, the changes were minimal. In an article written for *Time Magazine* in 1952, the then elder statesman of the movement concluded that teachers were more aware of the psychological development of their students and that "older gross manifestations . . . of education by fear and repression . . . have, generally speaking, been eliminated." However, he felt that "fundamental authoritarianism of the old education persists in various modified forms." Dewey believed, at least in 1952, that there was "little cooperative and democratic learning in American schools."[19]

While Dewey was disappointed with the impact of progressive ideas, there is solid evidence that inroads had been made in how students were being taught. In 1948, it was reported that 40 percent of the cities had "adopted some form of individualized instruction."[20] In every section of the country, there were public and private schools following to some degree the ideas of Dewey and his disciples. The pockets of reform could be found in one-room schools as well as in larger suburban and urban districts. Numerous private schools for children of all ages were experimenting with a large variety of new educational innovations. Not only at Teachers College at Columbia University, but at public and private teacher-training institutions throughout the country, professors were introducing progressive methods and theory to the next generation of teachers. Yet as we entered the 1950s, a counter-movement against these ideas was emerging. Although there are a number of factors and individuals who were responsible for this spirited attack against those supporting progressive education, perhaps the single most important catalyst for the critics was the surprise launching of a Russian space satellite known as Sputnik.

NOTES

1. Alfie Kohn, *The Schools Our Children Deserve*, (Boston: Houghton Mifflin Co., 1999), 6–7.

2. Joel Spring, *The American School: 1642–1990*, (New York: Longman, 1990), 179.

3. David B. Tyack, ed., *Turning Points in American Educational History*, (Malthan, MA: Blaisdell Publishing Company, 1967), 318–19.

4. David Tyack, Robert Lowe, and Elisabeth Hansot, *Public Schools in Hard Times*, (Cambridge, MA: Harvard University Press, 1984), 150.

5. Kohn, *The Schools Our Children Deserve*, 232.

6. Tyack, Lowe, and Henhsot, *Public Schools in Hard Times*, 155.

7. Tyack, Lowe, and Henhsot, *Public Schools in Hard Times*, 156–60.

8. Joel Spring, *American Education*, (Boston: McGraw-Hill, 2006), 275.

9. Spring, *American Education*, 275.

10. R. Freeman Butts and Lawrence A. Cremin, *A History of Education in American Culture*, (New York: Henry Holt and Co., 1953), 590.

11. Diane Ravitch, *Left Back: A Century of Battles Over School Reform*, (New York: Touchstone, 2000), 62.

12. Ravitch, *Left Back: A Century of Battles Over School Reform*, 67.

13. Robert F. McNergney and Joann M. Herbert, *Foundations of Education*, (Boston: Allyn and Bacon, 1998), 104.

14. L. Dean Webb, *The History of American Education*, (Upper Saddle River, NJ: Pearson Prentice Hall, 2006), 226.

15. Webb, *The History of American Education*, 226.

16. Webb, *The History of American Education*, 230.

17. John D. Pulliam and James J. Van Patten, *History of Education in America*, (Upper Saddle River, NJ: Merrill, 1991), 181.

18. Frederick Mayer, *American Ideas and Education*, (Columbus, OH: Charles E. Merrill Books, Inc. 1964), 392.

19. Spring, *The American School: 1642–1990*, 269.

20. Butts and Cremin, *A History of Education in American Culture*, 590.

5

The Fifties

The major wave of criticism of progressive education theory actually began prior to the launch of Sputnik in 1957. Historian Diane Ravitch put it
in the bluntest of terms when she wrote "the 1950's was a horrible decade
for progressive educators."[1] Another historian used the word "vitriolic"
when describing the attacks on progressive educators.[2] Supporters of progressive educational theory were equally emotional in describing some of
the critics "as a motley assortment of 'chronic tax conservationists,' 'con-
genital reactionaries,' 'witch hunters,' 'super patriots,' 'dogma peddlers,'
'race haters,' and last but not least, 'academic conservatives.'"[3]

As in other eras in American history, the educational conflict in the
1950s was part of larger historical trends. At the end of World War II,
government planners were worried about a return to the high unemployment of the depression years. With hundreds of thousands of veterans returning, there was a concern that the economy would not be able to ab-
sorb them all into the workforce. In planning for the postwar period, there
developed a conviction by some federal government officials and business leaders that the leadership of progressive school administrators during the previous decade had made schools "anti-intellectual." For these
critics there was not enough attention being paid to the basic subjects of
English, history, math, and science. This feeling would be reinforced late
in the fifties when the Russians beat the United States in the space race
by launching the first missile into space. Even more damaging was the

charge by some ultraconservatives that education "had been infiltrated by communists." The ongoing reality of the Cold War, which would dominate U.S. foreign policy for decades, also created pressure on schools to train more scientists to ensure that our nation was victorious in the arms race with Russia.[4]

There were numerous critics during the fifties who found fault with the theory of progressive educators. An overriding theme among these individuals was that schools had strayed from their basic purpose. Richard Hofsteader, an American historian who has written extensively about how philosophy and ideas have shaped American history, wrote in 1953 that "American education today is in the midst of a great crisis . . . an inner failure of nerve." This has caused educators to forget "the importance and value of the life of the mind." There has been "a capitulation within the educational world—indeed, in many quarters an eager capitulation—to the non-intellectual or anti-intellectual" forces in our society.[5] He suggests that there is a "widespread distrust of intellectuals in America." Because of this, Hofsteader concluded that what has happened in our schools and colleges has been that "within only a few decades, a curriculum system that had been too tight and too rigid was made too loose and too sprawling. All kinds of practical skills that had neither professional nor intellectual stature—no matter how necessary they might be to the community— were taught, or presumed to be taught," within our schools and universities.[6]

It is this same issue that led American historian Arthur Bestor to launch his attack on schools. His best-selling books would affect the thinking of parents and school boards throughout the nation. In 1953, several years before Sputnik, Bestor published his first book of criticism, titled *Educational Wastelands*. His critique of the earlier progressive initiatives was that they had "set forth purposes of education so trivial as to forfeit the respect of thoughtful men and by deliberately divorcing the schools from the disciplines of science and scholarship." What he sought was a return to the basic liberal arts curriculum. He would write in 1956, that the curricula in our schools should be "systematic and sequential" because "clear thinking is systematic thinking" and "liberal education involves the logical organization of knowledge." Later in his career, Bestor would become one of the founders of the Council on Basic Education.[7] In this capacity, he would claim that "concern with the personal problems of adolescents had grown so excessive as to push into the background what should be the school's central concern, the intellectual development of its students."[8]

In his attacks, Bestor was especially hard on those he called "the interlocking directorate of professional educationists." He points to earlier years when academic scholars were considered to be the authorities on what should be taught in schools. It was his feeling that this was no longer the case. In part, he blamed university professors, who "tended to turn their backs upon elementary and secondary education." This, along with the development of pedagogy as an independent subject in the university curriculum, resulted in turning over curriculum decisions to the "professional educationists." According to Bestor, this occurred gradually as education professors who were committed to collaboration with other academic departments were replaced by a new generation of education professors who received almost all of their academic training from colleges of education. Bestor believed that this converted college teacher training programs into a form of "vocational education." Teachers were entering elementary and secondary classrooms with training in progressive teaching methods but with a very weak background in the liberal arts. He blamed this trend on the professors of education, who, along with school administrators, ignored the school's responsibility to what Bestor believed to be the basic subjects of the curriculum. What he was saying during the 1950s would be echoed by the proponents of the academic standards movement in the late 1980s.[9] To a lesser degree it is beginning to be heard as well during the first decade of the twenty-first century.

A second critic during the 1950s was Admiral Hyman Rickover, who believed that the outcome of the Cold War with Russia was dependent on the reform of education in the United States. He was especially concerned about improving the teaching of science in our schools.[10] A true supporter of the "back to basics movement," he believed that "education involves perspiration and not play or social activities."[11] In his book *Education and Freedom* (1956), Rickover raised the question of "why Johnny could not read while Ivan could." For him, at least, it was the lack of basic skills training that was hindering our nation's ability to compete with Russia and the only solution was to have our schools return to emphasizing basic skills. We needed a "de-emphasis of life-adjustment schools and progressive educationists" and a return to an emphasis on science and math.[12]

Rickover's concern with our Cold War competition with Russia was shared in another best-selling book released in the 1950s, *The Big Red Schoolhouse*. The author, Fred M. Hechinger, begins the book by referring to a CBS program that profiled a typical Russian student named Ivan. The boy spoke English well and was very diligent about his homework. After hearing a description of this typical Russian teenager, some students in Tennessee were interviewed on camera and asked to share their thoughts about Ivan. The consensus of these American students was that "too much work had undoubtedly made Ivan a dull boy." One American girl shared her opinion that much of what Ivan was studying was a waste of time and that he would most likely be a dull date. When asked what the most important thing students needed to learn in school was, the American students agreed that it was "how to get along with other people."[13] Hechinger ends his book with these words of caution, "history plays strange tricks. The United States was built by men and women whose traditions were deeply rooted in the European past of scholarship and learning." As we developed as a nation, we also accepted the unprecedented goal of providing an equal educational opportunity for all children. Somehow, this new ideal caused us to forget our commitment to scholarship and academic excellence. In fact, "some of the spokesmen for education began to hint that excellence was an undemocratic discrimination. It is the irony of history that it took the Russians to remind us, not only that excellence is an indispensable ingredient for survival, but that a lazy democracy is a dying democracy."[14]

Although Hechinger's book was nonfiction, even the novels of the decade lauded traditional teachers. In Frances Gray Patton's book *Good Morning, Miss Dove*, the heroine, Miss Dove, was anything but a progressive educator. Her rules "were as fixed as the signs of the Zodiac. And they were known. . . . It was Miss Dove's experience that the eight-year-old mind learned best by rote."[15] In the novel, the author undoubtedly supports teachers like Miss Dove. This is evident as the reader is told:

> Occasionally, a group of progressive mothers would contemplate organized revolt. "She's been teaching too long," they would cry. "Her pedagogy hasn't changed since we were in Cedar Grove. She rules the children through fear!" They would turn to the boldest one among themselves. "You go," they would say. "You go talk to her!" The bold one would go, but somehow she never did much talking. Without firing a shot in the cause of freedom, she would retreat ingloriously from the field of battle.[16]

Another classic novel about a teacher, published in 1963, was *Goodbye, Mr. Chips* by James Hilton. This book also portrayed a traditional teacher in a private boys' school in England. The book and the movie telling the story of this traditional teacher of Latin and Greek provided an admirable role model for teachers around the world. Even one of the most-viewed movies of the period, *Blackboard Jungle*, suggested the need for more discipline in our public high schools.

It was neither movies nor books that provided the primary impetus for the negative reaction against progressive education during the 1950s. For many Americans, including some prominent national leaders, the single event that caused them to begin to doubt the effectiveness of our schools was the Russian triumph in space. After the launching of Sputnik in 1958, it was only a few months before Congress would pass a major federal aid program for our schools. It was called The National Defense Education Act, and it offered financial aid to states and school districts to improve their programs in science, math, and foreign languages.[17] The legislation also set into motion training opportunities for teachers and several national curriculum projects designed to increase the academic rigor of high school courses.[18]

The media as well as several prominent books tended to suggest that our problems in the space race were at least in part caused by our ineffective public schools. Americans were told that our schools had "gone soft" and that instruction in subject-matter content compared unfavorably with that provided to students in other countries.[19] For some of our national leaders, our public education system had become a "weapon" in the Cold War.[20] Historian L. Dean Webb has written that the Sputnik challenge caused the nation to suddenly care about intelligence, especially in science and math. To many, "progressive education seemed out of step."[21]

Continuing into the early sixties, the criticism did not let up. In a 1961 article for *Fortune*, Charles E. Silberman would tell those who read this influential business magazine that "for two generations, intellectual training has not been the main goal of the U.S. public school system; indeed, it has never been the main goal of any school system designed for the broad mass of a population."[22] In speaking about what had happened in our schools, he suggested that progressive education did meet some needs as our nation began the twentieth century and for fifty years, these theories helped our country make the "difficult transition from farming to an industrial society, at the same time absorbing and Americanizing the children of millions of immigrants. 'Adjustment' was what the American school child needed—and the schools of yesterday supplied it."[23] He goes on to argue that:

> The U.S. today is moving away from progressivism not because it is "false" in some absolute sense, but because it badly serves the needs of our own time. The growing complexity of organization and the explosive pace of technological and social change are creating an enormous demand that is without historical precedent.
>
> Public schools have been wasting valuable years by postponing the teaching of many important subjects on the grounds that they are too difficult. In fact, the basic ideas of science and mathematics, and the basic themes of literature and history should form the heart of the curriculum from the elementary grades on.[24]

He concludes this 1961 article by expressing his belief that the nation needed to move away from the theories of the progressive educators and adopt a "back to basics" approach.

This was the view of perhaps a majority of Americans, at least for the next several years. In a recent article in the *Wilson Quarterly*, "The Other Sixties," Bruce Bawer writes about the interlude between 1959 and 1965. It was a time when our nation was moving from the dominant conservative views of the fifties to the somewhat radical thoughts that affected the late sixties and early seventies. He points out that to those on the right of the political spectrum, the fifties were "the last good time, an era of sanity and maturity, order and discipline, of adults behaving like adults and children knowing their place." On the other hand, "to those on the left, the 1950s were a time of fatuous complacency, mindless materialism, and stultifying conformism—not to mention racism, sexism, and other ugly prejudices." The tables were turned in the sixties that conservatives would see as an "explosion of puerile irresponsibility and fashionable rebellion, the wellspring of today's ubiquitous identity politics, debased high culture, sexual permissiveness, and censorious political correctness." Liberals, on the other hand, were happier during the sixties, as they saw the period as a time of "desperately needed correction that drew attention to

America's injustices and started us down the road toward greater fairness and equality for all."[25]

In this article, Bawer argued that the years of the Kennedy administration (1961–1963) were a decent and earnest interlude that ended on November 22, 1963, with the assassination of the president. He concludes his article by telling how he personally experienced the beginning of the sixties. It was at nightfall on November 22, while walking in a park in Queens, New York, that he "saw a teenage boy with shoulder-length hair." For others it might have been a time when they:

> first smelled a strange, sickly sweet smoke coming from the back of the school bus. On that day when he walked in the park, he saw young people dressed in T-shirts and bell-bottom jeans, one or two of them playing guitar, their manner was strangely causal, loose, relaxed in a way I had never seen before. And, yes, with flowers in their hair.
>
> I didn't know what to make of them. But their image lodged firmly in my mind, and I knew that the world had changed.[26]

This change would be felt strongly as well, in the field of education. Schools would be in the forefront in this new and very different era known as the sixties.

NOTES

1. Diane Ravitch, *Left Back: A Century of Battles Over School Reform*, (New York: Touchstone, 2000), 361.

2. Robert F. McNergney and Joann M. Herbert, *Foundations of Education*, (Boston: Allyn and Bacon, 1998), 117.

3. Lawrence A. Cremmin, *The Transformation of the School*, (New York: Alfred A. Knopf, 1964), 342–43.

4. Joel Spring, *The American School: 1642–1990*, (New York: Longman, 1990), 323–24.

5. Stan Dropkin, Harold Full, and Ernest Schwarcz, *Contemporary American Education*, (New York, Macmillan Company, 1965), 168.

6. Dropkin, Full, and Schwarcz, *Contemporary American Education*, 183.

7. L. Dean Webb, *The History of American Education*, (Upper Saddle River, NJ: Pearson Prentice Hall, 2006), 263.

8. Allan C. Ornstein, *Pushing the Envelope, Critical Issues in Education*, (Upper Saddle River, NJ: Merrill Prentice Hall, 2003), 84.

9. Ronald S. Brandt, ed., *Education in a New Era*, (Alexandria: The Association for Supervision and Curriculum Development, 2000), 15.

10. Mortimer J. Adler and Milton Mayer, *The Revolution in Education*, (Chicago: University of Chicago Press, 1958), 93.

11. Ornstein, *Pushing the Envelope, Critical Issues in Education*, 296.

12. Ornstein, *Pushing the Envelope, Critical Issues in Education*, 84.

13. Fred M. Hechinger, *The Big Red Schoolhouse*, (Garden City, NY: Doubleday & Company, Inc., 1959), 26.

14. Hechinger, *The Big Red Schoolhouse*, 235.

15. Roselle K. Chartock, *Educational Foundations*, (Upper Saddle River, NJ: Merrill, 2000), 288–89.

16. Chartock, *Educational Foundations*, 288.

17. Madonna M. Murphy, *The History and Philosophy of Education*, (Upper Saddle River, NJ: Pearson, 2006), 324.

18. David G. Armstrong, Kenneth T. Henson, and Tom V. Savage, *Education: An Introduction*, (New York: MacMillian Publishing Co., Inc., 1981), 60.

19. Armstrong, Henson, and Savage, *Education: An Introduction*, 39.

20. Webb, *The History of American Education*, 243.

21. Webb, *The History of American Education*, 264.

22. Leonard Freedman, *Issues of the Sixties*, (Belmont, CA: Wadsworth Publishing Company, Inc., 1966), 406.

23. Freedman, *Issues of the Sixties*, 408.

24. Freedman, *Issues of the Sixties*, 408–409.

25. Bruce Bawer, "The Other Sixties," *Wilson Quarterly*, XXVIII, no. 2, Spring 2004, 64.

26. Bawer, "The Other Sixties," 84.

6

The Sixties and Seventies

Although many observers believed that progressive education had seen its day by the end of the fifties, national and international events would soon conspire to bring about what certainly seemed to be a rebirth in the movement. Diane Ravitch has written that in 1963 and 1964, "the post-Sputnik enthusiasm for academic improvement abruptly ended, and was replaced as the leading national topic by the urban crisis."[1] In 1963, author George F. Kneller would predict that:

> We may be confident that the present decline of progressivism is only temporary. The movement, like all such movements, will take on life again in fresher and more vigorous forms. By drawing attention to the currents of change and renewal that run constantly through the universe and through education itself, and by continually challenging the existing order, progressivism expresses an educational attitude of abiding significance.[2]

Perhaps it was the assassination of John Kennedy in November of 1963 that was the first of a series of events that would effect a change in the conservative focus of the fifties. The loss of the nation's young president was a significant event for most Americans. People of all ages can remember exactly where they were and what they were doing that November day and perhaps throughout the entire weekend. Five years later, the deaths of Martin Luther King Jr. and Robert Kennedy, as well as the ongoing protests against the Vietnam War, would plunge the United States into an even more violent turmoil. In 1968, citizens also would watch on television as the Chicago police used tear gas and their nightsticks on protestors during the Democratic Convention. Other cities were also experiencing violence as there was a nationwide uprising by African-American citizens who were seeking equal rights.

The seeds of the unrest that characterized the sixties were sown with the 1954 court decision in the case of Brown vs. Topeka, Kansas. This landmark case initiated what would be a gradual attempt to ensure integration in our schools. Later, this civil rights struggle would widen as the movement for equal rights for women also emerged as a major issue. Thrust into the presidency by the assassination of President Kennedy, Lyndon Johnson found himself facing a very organized and effective civil rights movement that included people of every race. While the most prominent civil rights leader, Martin Luther King Jr., taught and practiced peaceful protest, President Johnson was soon facing riots in a number of major cities. Although he was a lifelong resident of the conservative state of Texas, Johnson personally wanted very much to help the less fortunate in our society. Even before he became president, he would share his thoughts with a 1962 audience that:

> We have learned in the course of our work that the problem of equal opportunity is not confined solely to the availability of jobs. This question cannot be solved until we have not only equal opportunity in employment but equal opportunity and access to the training and action that qualifies men and women for the job.[3]

President Eisenhower and even President Kennedy had been reluctant to commit the federal government to a leadership role in fighting poverty and racial discrimination. President Johnson did not falter in moving forward in this area even though as a seasoned politician, he knew that his Democratic party would lose the support of many southern whites if it got too far ahead of public opinion on the civil rights issue. Of course, he was correct in this concern, and a large number of southerners have turned away from their historic support of the Democratic Party. One of the laws that most concerned some white southerners was the Voting Rights Bill of 1965. President Johnson made clear his own views on the issue in a speech to the House of Representatives when he said:

I speak tonight for the dignity of man and the destiny of democracy. . . . At times history and fate meet at a single time in a single place to shape a turning point in man's unending search for freedom. So it was at Lexington and Concord. So it was a century ago at Appomattox. So it was last week in Selma, Alabama. . . . There is no constitutional issue here. The command of the Constitution is plain. There is no moral issue . . . there is only the struggle for human rights. . . . This time, on this issue . . . there must be no delay, no hesitation, and no compromise with our purpose . . . because it is not just Negros, but really it is all of us who must overcome the crippling legacy of bigotry and injustice. And . . . we . . . shall . . . overcome.[4]

Even though the president had made it clear that he supported the civil rights movement, the integration of schools moved forward slowly. Busing programs appeared in many areas as the only way to break the segregation patterns brought on by the traditional commitment to neighborhood schools. Administrators and teachers in the schools not only had to deal with the new diverse pattern of their student bodies. but also with the need to provide appropriate educational opportunities for all of these children.

Schools were very much on the minds of the president and his advisors when they planned President Johnson's massive War on Poverty. Realizing that poverty was most frequently the result of a poor or incomplete education, Johnson believed that children from disadvantaged homes should be given an early boost. Because these children frequently lacked the educational, social, and medical benefits of middle-class children, there appeared to be a need to give three- and four-year-olds from poor families the type of preparation they would need to succeed in school. With this goal in mind, an integral part of the initiative against poverty was the Head Start program. The legislation that established the program was signed in 1965, and it opened the possibility for local communities to apply for federal funds to establish Head Start centers in their area. As a result of the legislation, programs for eligible families with low incomes were set up throughout the country. Along with preschool classes for the children, the students would also be eligible for health benefits. Parents were urged to attend parenting classes as the program attempted to give to students many of the advantages offered to their more affluent peers.

A larger and even more expensive federal initiative launched at the same time was the 1965 Elementary and Secondary Education Act. In the words of the president, the law was "a major new commitment of the federal government to quality and equality in schooling that we afford our young people."[5] The initial aid given to local school districts was over one billion dollars, and there were no requirements for matching funds by the state and local governments. There were five major sections of the law. By far, the largest expenditures of funds would be spent in the section of the legislation known as Title I. This portion of the law was designed to provide funds to districts based on the number of poor children they were educating. This section of the law would utilize 80 percent of the total funds allocated by the legislation for remedial programs. It was intended to supplement the Head Start program by seeing that poor children continued to receive the help they needed when they entered their local school district. In schools throughout the country, additional teachers were hired to provide remedial reading and math instruction to eligible children. When this same Title I program was considered for reauthorization in 2002, the revised law was called the No Child Left Behind Act. The Elementary and Secondary Act and Head Start would not be the last of the programs established by Congress to support public education. The idea was that the federal government would assist "those parts of schooling that appeared not to be receiving support by the local governments."[6]

The emergence of the federal government as a player in funding and managing our public schools along with the poverty program and the civil rights struggle were all factors that disturbed the status quo in our schools in the 1960s. As the decade proceeded, the growing war in Vietnam would become an overriding concern of the American people. After the passage of the Civil Rights bills and the assassinations of Martin Luther King Jr. and Robert Kennedy in 1968, the Vietnam War and student demonstrations replaced other stories on the front pages of our newspapers. Unfortunately, the cost of the war adversely affected the funding for the War on Poverty. The unpopularity of the war also was a primary factor in causing President Johnson to give up any plans to seek reelection in 1968. This, along with the election of the more conservative Richard Nixon, would further slow additional federal initiatives in civil rights, poverty programs, and federal aid to education.

As public debates and demonstrations erupted throughout the nation on college campuses, schools would also feel the divisiveness of the war. High school students joined their older friends in demonstrations and teach-ins. Male high school students were very aware that their immediate future might include being drafted and sent to Vietnam. The student bodies of schools as well as members of individual families were often sharply divided on the question of the legitimacy of the Vietnam War. The popular media of the day was talking about a "generation gap." Bob Dylan would sing about the idea in his 1965 song, "The Times They Are a Changin'." One verse in the lyrics spoke directly to the youth rebellion and to the so-called "generation gap." Dylan would also write and sing about the fact that young people were breaking away from the conformity of the fifties when he wrote: "Your sons and your daughters / Are beyond your command."[7]

The spirit of rebellion and the need for change that was prominent in the popular culture also affected the field of education. In a book published in 1960, *The Future of Public Education*, Myron Lieberman discussed the problems facing schools and predicted "that within the next few decades, education from the U.S. will undergo changes of tremendous scope and magnitude."[8] The theme of a needed educational revolution was taken up later in the decade by Francis Keppel in his book, *The Necessary Revolution in American Education*. Keppel was very much caught up in the need to have equality in education, and at the same time, providing a "quality education" for all. He believed that we cannot have quality without true equality. In his own words, "perfectibility implies the ability for all to learn, and the duty of society to teach. The contemporary task is to make the doctrine real in the lives of all our children."[9] The question of the 1960s was, how do we achieve both quality and equality in our schools?

As early as 1959, education critic John Holt was worried about the overemphasis on traditional education methods and curriculum. He suggested "that children are too busy to think."[10] Five years later, Holt would trumpet the old progressive doctrine when he wrote:

> Most children in school fail. . . . They fail because they are afraid, bored, and confused . . . bored because the things they are given and told to do in school are so trivial, so dull, and make such limited and narrow demands on the wide spectrum of their intelligence, capabilities, and talents. . . . Schools should be a place where children learn what they want to know, instead of what we think they ought to know.[11]

Holt and others were still fighting what they saw as the evils of traditional education a decade later when he wrote:

> Behind much of what we do in school lie some ideas that could be expressed roughly as follows: (1) Of the vast body of human knowledge, there are certain bits and pieces that can be called essential, . . . (2) the extent to which a person can be considered educated . . . depends on the amount of this essential knowledge that he carries about with him; (3) it is the duty of schools, therefore, to get as much of this essential knowledge as possible into the minds of children. . . . These ideas are absurd and harmful nonsense . . . children quickly forget all but a small part of what they learn in school. It is of no use or interest to them; they do not want, or expect, or even intend to remember it. The only difference between bad and good students in this respect is that the bad students forget right away, while the good students are careful to wait until after the exam.[12]

John Holt went beyond criticizing traditional education by writing several books including *What Do I Do on Monday?* to offer "practical suggestions to teachers about how to keep interest alive in schools and what can be done to encourage each student to reach his or her maximum potential."[13]

Other educators also were giving teachers specific ideas as to how to meet the goals of progressive education. In his book, *Thirty Six Children and the Open Classroom*, author Herbert Kohl tells us how he has created a curriculum using his students' experiences. Beginning in the 1960s, Jonathan Kozol began a crusade in which he has written a series of books to demonstrate the inequality of educational opportunity for poor children. In doing so, he has also offered "meaningful ideas for teaching children whose backgrounds are culturally different from those in the majority."[14]

The most radical of the critics during the decade was Ivan Illiach, who in his book, *Deschooling Society* (1971), advocated abolishing compulsory public education. A Roman Catholic priest until 1961, he believed that "schools are used as screening devices to sift out the gifted few or justify the existence of high schools and colleges for the children of the wealthy and powerful." He did not think that it was possible to create public schools that could "actually meet the needs of the masses." If we as a nation did away with schools, "there would no longer be power or prestige associated with staying in school a long time or acquiring a degree."[15] Of the educational critics who were writing during the 1960s, Peter

Scherg would write in *The Saturday Review*, that they all had the "common view" that "a hostile society and its educational system cripple and destroy the processes of learning, the dignity of youth, and the natural instincts of curiosity and self-realization." In addition he claimed that the critics believed that the current public schools were "coercive instruments designed to enforce conformity and deny self-esteem."[16]

Paul Goodman, who has been called, "the voice of the alienated college student and the leading statesman of the New Left," during the sixties would write that "the whole process of conventional education is brainwashing: The components are a uniform world-view, the absence of any viable alternative, confusion about the relevance of one's own experience and feelings, and a chronic anxiety, so that one clings to the one worldview as the only security. This is brainwashing."[17] Harkening back to Dewey and other early progressives, Goodman would write that "no growth to freedom occurs except by intrinsic motivation."[18] Peter Schrag concludes his essay on the educational critics of the sixties this way:

> The passions that followed Sputnik and the college panic divided us between those who wanted to make education a more efficient training instrument for the Cold War and middle-management, and those who resisted because the pap of life adjustment was more comfortable than intellectual rigor. The new critics have reminded us—sometimes, albeit, with too much wail—that relevant education has little to do with either, and that if it does not deal with the humanity of its students, it is not dealing with anything.[19]

One could go on talking about other individuals such as Carl Rogers and Neil Postman, both of whom were influential voices in calling for educational change during the sixties and seventies. As one looks back upon this period, it can be seen as a time when progressive education ideas reemerged in a slightly different format. One well-known model for school reform actually began long before the sixties, when A. S. Neill established the Summerhill School in England. A Summerhill society was formed in the United States and "during the student rebellions of the 1960s the Summerhill school was often cited as a model of alternative education." In these schools, it was claimed that "children would grow to be loving and happy adults." To accomplish this goal, the "children were given complete freedom to attend or not attend classes and were allowed to participate in the operation of the school."[20]

Some American schools were affected by this approach during the sixties and seventies. Students were asked to participate on high school advisory committees and some were allowed to become members of the board of education. Many secondary schools gave students free time where they had previously been assigned to a mandatory study hall. These students were allowed to move freely about the building, and in some schools, student lounges were established. Here the young people could relax or play a game of ping-pong. Other schools introduced smoking lounges for students. Perhaps the most far-reaching change occurred when some communities allowed their students to leave campus during their free time. This so-called "open campus" system might be granted only to older students as it was introduced in the hope that it would help to prepare them for the additional freedom they would experience in college life.

During this period, curriculums were altered as part of an effort to meet the students' desire for a more "relevant" curriculum. For many high schools, this led to the introduction of new electives. This was especially true in social studies, where classes in sociology, politics, and economics challenged the dominance of history. In some states, American history became American Studies, and the chronological approach gave way to a topical curriculum emphasizing the social sciences. Other schools introduced electives such as Problems of Democracy. There also were new courses introduced in other curricular areas. During the energy crisis of the early seventies, students were introduced to classes in ecology and some schools celebrated "Earth Day" with mini-electives. English electives sometimes replaced the traditional English classes. Students were allowed to choose from options such as Science Fiction Literature, Adventure Literature, Sports Literature, or classes devoted solely to women or African-American authors.

Another trend of the period was to combine several subjects into a single class that might be called Humanities. Such a class could be team taught by a history, English, art, and perhaps a music teacher. Other liberal communities actually introduced alternative schools as part of the public schools system. Minneapolis, for instance, included schools utilizing the Summerhill philosophy.[21] In some cases, these alternative schools were opened in the hope that by giving students and parents the choice, it would help to break up the segregation caused by neighborhood schools. In time, these alternative schools would assume the name of magnet schools and would provide parents and students with an array of options in larger districts. As the magnet concept developed, the options went beyond offering progressive schools. A school was given a particular focus, such as science or the arts. Today, although there might be one or two schools in a district that are built upon the progressive education theory, most magnet schools are quite traditional in their approach.

Some elementary schools were also affected by the desire to experiment during the late sixties and seventies. The so-called open classroom or open school was a popular innovation during the period. The open classroom sought to utilize "student-directed learning as opposed to teacher-determined instruction." Active learning was the goal rather than passive teacher-centered learning. In such a classroom or school, children were expected to "plan their own learning and move from interest station to interest station."[22] Both elementary and secondary schools were built without the many walls that separated learning spaces in the traditional school building. The idea of learning centers devoted to specific subjects was very popular as areas in the larger rooms would be created for students to engage in "hands-on work" in different subject areas. Children might spend time classifying plants at the science learning center and then move on to work with historical relics or documents at the social studies center. A comfortable reading corner might be provided for students to read silently.

Another educational reform affecting elementary schools that created great conflict in the decades during this time period was the introduction of the whole language method of teaching language arts. For decades children were taught to read and write using basal readers, which were grade-level reading books made up of short stories. There was a heavy emphasis on using phonics to recognize and pronounce words that were unfamiliar to the student. They were taught to pronounce words by using long and short versions of vowels. Students also worked in separate workbooks designed to reinforce phonics and grammar rules. A third book was used to teach spelling and exercises in this book also might include phonetic drills. When students were given compositions to write, the topics were usually ones chosen by the instructor. For instance, during the first week of school, children might be asked to write about what they did during their summer vacation.

Supporters of whole language felt that traditional methods tended to segregate language arts skills, and that the basal readers and workbooks were often boring and uninspiring for children. They believed that students "acquire language through actually using it for a purpose, not through practicing its separate parts." By concentrating on the very best children's literature for the basis of the curriculum, students could be stimulated and motivated to love reading and be saved from the dullness that critics felt was inherent in the traditional system. Spelling words and writing assignments were to be taken primarily from the literature chosen by the teacher. In this way, the language arts curriculum could be unified rather than be taught in separate segments. Classroom libraries would be created, and students would be encouraged to read books of their choice. It was thought that the more often students could be encouraged to read and write on their own, the more quickly they would be able to master the necessary skills. Whole language teachers would de-emphasize phonics and teach their students to use the context in which the words were found to identify them. While the students were learning to write, teachers were encouraged to allow "inventive" spelling and to avoid frustrating writers by putting too many red marks on their written work. The idea was to focus on "meaning, not the component parts of language." English skills would be taught as a unified whole, rather than in separate approaches. Finally, the hope was that students "would have some control over learning." In doing so, they would be "more motivated and retain what they learn longer."[23]

The conflict between those supporting whole language and those favoring traditional methods for teaching language arts has gone on for decades. It has caused fierce debates in individual schools, boards of education meetings, and even in state legislative bodies. In California, it was a subject of a special referendum put before the voters of the state. Thought of by many conservatives as an outgrowth of progressive education, by the late eighties, whole language was being attacked on many fronts. Calls for a return to the teaching of phonics were heard throughout the nation. Still, few would question that this debate has introduced into our nation's classrooms a more diverse approach to this essential element of our school curriculum.

The educational trends during the sixties and seventies were not without their critics. During the Administration of Richard Nixon (1969–1974), there were fierce conservative reactions "to student demonstrations and the demands of the civil rights movement."[24] Historian Joel Spring described the ideas of these critics as "a retreat from the programs of the War on Poverty . . . career education . . . and a renewed emphasis on the power of the educational expert, the spread of the concept of accountability in education, and increased emphasis on testing."[25] As president, Nixon reduced federal spending on education, arguing that there was little evidence that the programs begun under President Johnson were having a positive effect on academic achievement. Backing away from federal aid to education was justified in part by the report of James Coleman of Johns Hopkins University, whose conclusions were simplified by some who interpreted them as saying that "nothing could be done in the schools to increase achievement among the lower class and, therefore, that such efforts were not worth the spending of federal dollars."[26] At the same time, the Nixon Administration was also backing away from schemes involving bussing students to achieve racial integration.

The reforms of these two decades have been characterized as part of the pendulum phenomenon that has been part of our educational history. The fact that opinions continually change can be understood "in part, at least, because the truths and children's learning are very complex, and in part because we are a very faddish culture." Author Joseph Featherstone wrote in his 1976 book *What Schools Can Do* that "the recent wave of informal, open classroom reform has not always been a success, but it has made more parents and teachers conscious of the realm of educational practice." Featherstone goes on to say that he believes that this has caused many to conclude "that variety in education is a good thing." While he would also agree that even though the educational fads of the period might "come and go," they might well have caused many "thoughtful people . . . to question the traditional tendency of schools to treat children as passive objects of education, and teachers as passive conduits of curriculum and policy."[27]

Others expressed serious reservations concerning educational initiatives undertaken during the sixties. In his book *Open Education and the American School*, published in 1972, Rowland S. Barth described "his own disastrous effort to introduce open education into two inner-city public schools with mainly Black enrollment." As a result of this experiment, Barth concluded that in his view what the children wanted was "stability and evidence of concern from their teachers." He would write "the open classrooms and their teachers provided neither. . . . Children tested and

⌐ every teacher who was attempting to run an unfamiliar classroom, until the teacher demanded conventional order or was run out and another came to take his place."[28]

At the same time books criticizing innovations in education were being published, the public was being informed of the declining Scholastic Aptitude Test scores. In 1975, it was announced that these scores had been dropping since the 1963–1964 school year. Another blue ribbon panel was vehement in their criticism of a practice that was labeled "social promotion." Many school districts had eliminated the practice of retaining students at a grade level because they failed to meet academic expectations. This practice too was blamed on progressive educators who were too focused on the "self esteem" of students. Others began to point to the reduction in enrollments in academic courses at the high school level as well as what seemed to be a lowering of academic standards in these classes. There were also surveys that pointed to the fact that students seemed to be spending considerably less time on homework. A commission appointed by President Jimmy Carter joined the criticism of schools when it concluded that, "Americans' incompetence in foreign languages is nothing short of scandalous, and it is even becoming worse." The report also showed a marked decline in enrollment in language courses between 1965 and 1979.[29]

All of these criticisms in the late seventies foreshadowed what would become a major call for a return to schools that saw their primary role as providing an excellent academic education to our nation's students. The single event which perhaps more than any other would motivate significant changes in our educational priorities was the issuance in 1983 of the *A Nation at Risk* report.

NOTES

1. Diane Ravitch, *Left Back: A Century of Battles Over School Reform*, (New York: Touchstone, 2000), 383.

2. Editor George F. Kneller, *Foundations of Education*, (New York: John Wiley and Sons, Inc.), 108.

3. Lyndon Baines Johnson, *The Vantage Point*, (New York: Holt, Rinehart, and Winston, 1971), 156.

4. Ravitch, *Left Back: A Century of Battles Over School Reform*, 165.

5. L. Dean Webb, *The History of American Education*, (Upper Saddle River, NJ: Pearson Prentice Hall, 2006), 285.

6. Joel Spring, *American Education*, (Boston: McGraw-Hill, 1998), 214.

7. http://bobdylan.com/songs/times.html. (accessed 20 October 2005), 1.

8. Myron Lieberman, *The Future of Public Education*, (Chicago: University of Chicago Press, 1960), 2.

9. Francis Keppel, *The Necessary Revolution in American Education*, (New York: Harper and Row Publishers, 1966), 11.

10. Alfie Kohn, *The Schools Children Deserve*, (Boston: Houghton Mifflin Co., 1999), 21.

11. Jack L. Nelson, Stuart B. Palonsky, and Mary Rose McCarthy, *Critical Issues in Education*, (Boston: McGraw Hill, 2004), 20.

12. Nelson, Palonsky, and McCarthy, *Critical Issues in Education*, 244.

13. John D. Pulliam and James J. Van Patten, *History of Education in America*, (Upper Saddle River, NJ: Merrill, 1995), 212.

14. Pulliam and Van Patten, *History of Education in America*, 213.

15. Pulliam and Van Patten, *History of Education in America*, 212–13.

16. Stan Dropkin, Harold Full, and Ernest Schwarcz, *Contemporary American Education*, (London: The Macmillan Company, 1970), 265–66.

17. Dropkin, Full, Schwarcz, *Contemporary American Education*, 267–68.

18. Dropkin, Full, Schwarcz, *Contemporary American Education*, 270.

19. Dropkin, Full, Schwarcz, *Contemporary American Education*, 274.

20. Joel Spring, *The American School: 1642–1990*, (New York: Longman, 1990), 367.

21. Spring, *The American School: 1642–1990*, 368.

22. Spring, *American Education*, 248.

23. Authur K. Ellis and Jeffery T. Fouts, *Research on Educational Innovations*, (Larchmont, NY: Eye on Education, Inc., 1997), 113.

24. Don Kauchak, Paul Eggen, and Mary D. Burbank, *Charting a Professional Course*, (Upper Saddle River, NJ: Pearson, 2005), 297.

25. Joel Spring, *The American School: 1642–1985*, (New York: Longman, 1986), 314.

26. Spring, *The American School: 1642–1985*, 314.

27. Spring, *The American School: 1642–1985*, 319.

28. Joseph Featherstone, *What Schools Can Do*, (Toronto: Liveright Publishing Corporation, 1976), 5.

29. Ravitch, *Left Back: A Century of Battles Over School Reform*, 400.

A Nation at Risk (1983)

Some observers have compared the impact of the *A Nation at Risk* report in the 1980s to that of the launching of Sputnik during the fifties.[1] Both caused a heightened focus on the need to reform our schools. The results were similar in that both led to efforts to return to an emphasis on basic curriculum subjects. Although the initiatives during the fifties did perhaps improve the teaching of science in our schools, the events of the sixties intervened and there were few major changes that took place in the period immediately after Sputnik. This has not been the case with the *A Nation at Risk* report. We now can see a number of significant trends that have emerged in our system of public education as a result of this national study. Many of the developments during the past twenty years can be traced directly to the recommendations of the report, which one textbook claims "galvanized Americans, moving education to center stage."[2]

Many others have written about the historic importance of the report. Historian Diane Ravitch describes it this way:

> *A Nation at Risk* was a landmark of education reform literature. Countless previous reports by prestigious national commissions had been ignored by the national press and the general public. *A Nation at Risk* was different. Written in stirring language that the general public could understand, the report warned that schools had not kept pace with the changes in society and the economy and the nation would suffer if education were not dramatically improved for all children. It also asserted that lax academic standards were

correlated with lax behavior standards and that neither should be ignored. *A Nation at Risk* was a call to action.[3]

The late Albert Shanker, the well-known former president of the American Federation of Teachers, was quoted ten years after the report came out that it had been "an exposition of what we could now call 'systematic reform': figuring out what we want students to know and be able to do and making sure that all parts of the education system—standards, curriculum, textbooks, assessments, teacher training—move simultaneously toward the achievement of agreed-upon goals."[4] If one were to attempt to summarize the major movements that Albert Shanker was talking about during the years since 1983, they might include the following:

- The "back to basics" movement, which is an attempt to place more emphasis on English, math, science, history, and computer education
- The creation of curriculum standards in every major subject taught in our schools—these standards define what students should know and be able to do in every subject area
- The creation of "high-stakes testing" to ensure that students are truly learning what has been articulated in the curriculum standards
- The establishment of means to make schools accountable to the public for meeting the curriculum standards

These initiatives were launched because of the work of a federal education department that the Reagan Administration at the time wished to abolish. The Republican Party had taken the position that historically and constitutionally, education should be the province of state and local governments. President Reagan had not hidden his opinion that the federal government "did not solve problems, but that it was the problem." Even though it was very possible that his position might soon be eliminated, President Reagan's Secretary of Education, Terrel Bell, felt that the time was right for the creation of a distinguished panel to study the current educational scene and make recommendations that might improve our schools. An experienced educational administrator and federal government official, Secretary Bell ignored the fact that the White House was not interested in such a commission. Despite the opposition of some high-level presidential advisors, he personally selected a diverse combination of individuals to prepare a report to the American people on their schools.

The group was called the National Commission on Excellence, and it was chaired by Bell's friend, David Gardner, who for eighteen months would be appointed the president of the University of California. Also chosen for the Commission were representatives of business, higher education, school administrators, a representative of boards of education, and a public school teacher. The group would solicit research and hold public hearings in five different cities. Since the commission was made up of busy people, who all held responsible full-time jobs, a staff of sixteen federal workers was provided by Secretary Bell to help collect and collate the data. The mission statement prepared by the Secretary of Education asked that the study accomplish the following:

1. to review and synthesize the data and scholarly literature on the quality of learning and teaching in the nation's schools, colleges, and universities, both public and private, with special concern for educational experience of teen-age youth;
2. to examine and to compare and contrast the curricula, standards, and expectations of the educational systems of several advanced countries with those of the United States;
3. to study a representative sampling of university and college admission standards and lower division course requirements with particular reference to the impact upon the enhancement of quality and the promotion of excellence such standards may have on high school curricula and on expected levels of high school academic achievement;
4. to review and to describe educational programs that are recognized as preparing students who consistently attain higher than average scores in college entrance examinations and who meet with uncommon success the demands placed on them by the nation's colleges and universities;
5. to review the major changes that have occurred in American education as well as events in society during the past quarter century that have significantly affected educational achievement;
6. to hold hearings and to receive testimony and expert advice on efforts that could and should be taken to foster higher levels of quality and academic excellence in the nation's schools, colleges, and universities;
7. to do all other things needed to define the problems of and the barriers to attaining greater levels of excellence in American education;

8. to report and to make practical recommendations for action to be taken by educators, public officials, governing boards, parents, and others having a vital interest in American education and a capacity to influence it for the better.[5]

Beginning in August of 1981, the group did not complete its work until April of 1983. Along with the five public hearings, the group received twenty-six commissioned papers. Despite the diverse makeup of the Commission, the members were able to unanimously endorse the final report. During every decade, there are numerous national commissions that issue reports but most of them are soon forgotten. This one was different.

After President Reagan publicly released the document at a crowded press conference in the White House, the positive reaction pleasantly surprised both his staff and him. The report was immediately featured on news programs, on the radio and television, as well as in the printed media. It was a front-page story in most newspapers around the country, and some even printed it in its entirety. There were numerous editorials supporting its recommendations. Unlike many stories, it continued to be in the news for days, and both Secretary Bell and Chairman Gardner were guests on major news programs.[6]

The positive response was noted by the White House, and it was determined that it would be a popular issue during the president's campaign for reelection in 1984. As a result, on sixty-two occasions during the campaign, President Reagan selectively quoted from the report and supported its recommendations. After working hard to help reelect the President, Bell soon concluded that the Administration still lacked any sincere commitment to using the federal government to improve schools. For this reason he resigned from his position feeling "double-crossed." President Reagan told the press that Secretary Bell had resigned "for personal reasons."[7] Even with the resignation, the momentum for reform created by the report would be maintained by the state governors who would later meet together with Vice President Bush. Upon returning to their home states, they established commissions to move forward with reform. With strong encouragement from industrial leaders in every state, many of the initiatives suggested in the report were adopted.

The *A Nation at Risk* report was only one of many educational reports published during the 1980s, but somehow, more than any of the others, it touched a nerve in the American people. Its success, at least in part, can be attributed to the fact that the nation was troubled. When President Reagan began his Administration, the economy was in disarray. The national unemployment rate was at a post-depression high of 10.7 percent, while at the same time inflation was increasing at an annual rate of 12.5 percent. This unique condition was labeled "stagflation" and in order to control the rising prices, the Federal Reserve Board raised interest rates to an alarming 21.5 percent.[8]

At the same time, during the late seventies, the nation saw an increasing number of American businesses losing out to foreign competition. During this period the market share of our automobile and steel companies was declining rapidly. In looking for an explanation for our economic problems, there appeared to be a consensus among a number of influential business leaders that a primary problem was that the schools were failing to prepare a competitive workforce. Just as many had looked to the schools when we fell behind in the space race during the fifties, society was now prepared to focus on the education establishment as being a cause for the economic bad times facing the nation.

In stirring rhetoric, the introduction of the *A Nation at Risk* report would claim that:

> Our nation is at risk. Our once unchallenged prominence in commerce, industry, science, and technological innovation, is being overtaken by competitors throughout the world. . . . If an unfriendly foreign power had attempted to impose on America the mediocre educational performance that exists today, we might well have viewed it as an act of war. As it stands, we have allowed this to happen to ourselves. We have even squandered the gains in student achievement made in the wake of the Sputnik challenge. Moreover, we have dismantled essential support systems, which helped make those gains possible. We have, in effect, been committing an act of unthinking, unilateral educational disarmament.[9]

Had there not also been an underlying concern by many Americans about their schools and young people, the warning of the *A Nation at Risk* report would not have been taken so seriously. Diane Ravitch has written in her book, *Left Back*, that:

> By the early 1980s, there was growing concern about the quality of the nation's schools. The sustained assault on the academic curriculum in the late

60s and 70s had taken its toll. In 1980, the Gannett Newspaper chain sent investigative reporters into twenty-two schools in nine states, where they discovered that academic credit was offered for such courses as cheerleading, student government, and mass media. In the average school, students had only three hours each day of instructional time; students spent most of their time, even in their academic classes, on non-academic activities.[10]

The report itself focused on the lack of academic rigor in our high schools. After the introduction, it went on to point out what the Commission saw as the problems facing our schools. Called the Indicators of Risk, some of the more dramatic findings were:

- International comparisons of student achievement, completed a decade ago, reveal that on the nineteen academic tests, American students were never first or second, and, in comparison with other industrialized nations, were last seven times.
- Some twenty-three million American adults are functionally illiterate by the simplest test of everyday reading, writing, and comprehension.
- Average achievement of high school students on most standardized tests is now lower than twenty-six years ago when Sputnik was launched.
- College Board's Scholastic Aptitude Tests (SAT) demonstrate a virtually unbroken decline from 1963 to 1980. Average verbal scores fell over fifty points, and average mathematic scores dropped nearly forty points.
- There was a steady decline in science achievement scores of seventeen-year-olds in the United States as measured by national assessments of science in 1969, 1973, and 1977.
- Business and military leaders complain that they are required to spend millions of dollars on costly remedial education in training programs in such basic skills as reading, writing, spelling, and computation. The Department of the Navy, for example, reported to the Commission that one-fourth of its recent recruits cannot read at the ninth grade level, the minimum needed simply to understand written safety instructions. Without remedial work, they cannot even begin, much less complete, sophisticated training essential in much of the modern military.[11]

The report goes on to claim that "secondary school curricula homogenized, diluted, and diffused to the point that they no longer have a central purpose. In effect, we have a cafeteria-style curriculum in which the appetizers and desserts can easily be mistaken for the main courses."[12] Another deficiency noted was the dramatic decrease in homework. It was also pointed out that American students were spending only a fraction of the amount of time on math and science as students in competing countries. In thirteen states, students were able to take 50 percent or more of their coursework in electives. Textbooks, the Commission charged, were "written down" by publishers to lower and lower reading levels.

Another section discussed comparisons that were made on the time spent in school, and it was noted that in England, students spent eight hours a day for 220 days per year in school, while American students spend 180 days in school with each day lasting approximately six hours. The report also highlighted deficiencies in our teachers. For instance, the authors claimed that far too many of our teachers were being drawn from the bottom quarter of their high school class. It was also argued that students preparing to be teachers were taking too many education methods courses and too few content classes. In addition, the Commission stated its conclusion that teacher salaries were too low to attract the best and brightest people to the teaching profession. Finally, the national lack of qualified teachers in the field of math and science was noted.[13]

After outlining this exhaustive list of deficiencies in our schools, the report goes on to give a series of recommendations. This section begins by noting what the report lists as the "New Basics." It was the recommendation of the Commission that all high school students should be required to take the following courses during their four years in high school:

- Four years of English
- Three years of mathematics
- Three years of science
- Three years of social studies
- One-half year of computer science
- For college-bound students, two years of foreign language in high school are strongly recommended in addition to those taken earlier.[14]

The text goes on to call for "measurable standards" as well as "standardized tests of achievement" in the five basic subjects. It would be these recommendations that would eventually come to dominate the education reforms following the issuance of the *A Nation at Risk* report. To assist schools in teaching the New Basics, it was suggested that "textbooks and other tools for teaching and learning should be upgraded." After considering the instructional time spent in other countries, the Commission concluded that schools in the United States should dramatically increase both the time spent on instruction and on homework. It went on to suggest that state legislatures "strongly consider seven-hour school days as well as a school year which would include 200–220 days." To improve the caliber of individuals entering the teaching profession, the report recommends that outstanding teacher candidates be eligible for grants and loans to help pay for their education. This, along with higher salaries and chances of promotion within the profession (career ladders) were also included in the recommendations.[15]

The concept of school accountability was mentioned in the report. The authors noted that citizens across the nation should hold educators and elected officials accountable for providing the leadership necessary to achieve the reforms included in the report. Thus, the *A Nation at Risk* report did include a clear direction for what needed to be done to improve our schools. Among other initiatives, the report would clearly call for a movement back to basics, curriculum standards, high-stakes testing, school accountability, and improvements in the teaching profession.

The conservative nature of the recommendations of this and other reports criticizing public education during the 1980s were not universally applauded by either the media or all professional educators. Despite strong public support for much of the report, there were a number of vocal critics. During the month after the report was issued, there were twenty-eight articles in the *Washington Post* commenting on its content. Columnist Joseph Kraft saw the report as a chance for "conservatives" to "beat up liberals without offering anything constructive."[16] While some liberals were unhappy, well-known conservative William Buckley considered the recommendations "unimaginative" and "banal" because they offered nothing new. Even the writing was criticized by *New York Times* humor columnist Russell Baker, who gave the authors of the report "A+ for mediocrity."[17]

Historian Lawrence Cremin challenged the re
tion's economic problems on the schools as he su;
that the problems of international competitivene:
cational reform, especially educational reform de:
form, is not merely utopian . . . is at best a foolisl
fort to direct attention away from those truly
something about competitiveness. . . . It is a device that has been used re-
peatedly in the history of American education."[18]

Still others took issue with much of the data used by the authors to paint
the dismal view of what was happening in our schools. For instance, it
was pointed out that although SAT scores had indeed declined, the number of students taking these exams had increased dramatically. No longer
was it just the top high school students who took the test, but a much
larger sampling.[19] It was also suggested that there was other data that
could have been used leading to more positive conclusions and that even
the studies included, it was charged, had "fundamental, methodological
flaws."[20]

Jonathan Kozol and others, while complimenting the report on bring-
ing the issue of public education to the forefront, believed that the authors had not focused on the most important problem. For Kozol, the
primary issue has always been the fact that our system does not truly
offer equal opportunity to all students. Because of the way we finance
education, children who live in our poorest urban and rural areas are
denied the same opportunities as young people attending schools in the
wealthy suburbs.[21]

While there were many who doubted the value of the *A Nation at Risk*
report, the general public was mostly unaware of the dissenting views. As
a result in states and communities, efforts were launched to move forward
in implementing many of the recommendations. The ideas that were associated throughout the twentieth century with progressive education
were not in the forefront of the reforms that were to occur. In fact, during
the past twenty years, it is possible to conclude that progressive education,
as it was defined by John Dewey and other pioneers during the first half
of the twentieth century, and again in the sixties, had ceased to be a major
force in American education. To understand why one might believe this to
be the case, it is necessary to consider the events that have shaped our
schools during the past twenty years.

NOTES

1. John D. Pulliam and James J. Van Patten, *History of Education in America,* (Upper Saddle River, NJ: Merrill, 1995), 235.

2. Myra Pollack Sadker and David Miller Sadker, *Teachers, Schools, and Society, 6th Edition*, (Boston: McGraw Hill, 2003), 149.

3. Diane Ravitch, *Left Back: A Century of Battles Over School Reform*, (New York: Touchstone, 2000), vii.

4. David T. Gordon, editor, *A Nation Reformed?*, (Cambridge, MA: Harvard Education Press, 2003), 2.

5. U.S. Department of Education, The National Commission on Excellence in Education, *A Nation at Risk: The Imperative for Educational Reform*, April, 1983, app. A, 1–2.

6. Terrel H. Bell, *The Thirteenth Man*, (New York: The Free Press, 1988), 28–32.

7. Wilbur Edel, *The Reagan Presidency: An Actor's Finest Performance*, (New York: Hippocrene Books, 2000), 134.

8. Time-Life Books, *Pride and Prosperity: The 80's*, (Alexandria, VA: Time-Life Books, 1999), 24–26.

9. Sadker and Sadker, *Teachers, Schools, and Society, 6th Edition*, 148.

10. Ravitch, *Left Back: A Century of Battles Over School Reform*, 408.

11. U.S. Department of Education, The National Commission on Excellence in Education, *A Nation at Risk*: The Imperative for Educational Reform, April 1983, Introduction, 3.

12. Gordon, *A Nation Reformed?*, 179.

13. Gordon, *A Nation Reformed?*, 179–83.

14. Gordon, *A Nation Reformed?*, 184.

15. Gordon, *A Nation Reformed?*, 186–88.

16. Gerald W. Bracey, "April Foolishness: The 20th Anniversary of a Nation at Risk," *Phi Delta Kappan,* April 2003, www.pdkintl.org/kappan/k0304bra.htm (accessed 4 November 2005), 4.

17. Bracey, "April Foolishness," 5.

18. Lawrence J. Cremin, *Popular Education and its Discontents*, (New York: Harper & Row, 1989), 102–103.

19. Ray Marshall and Marc Tucker, *Thinking for a Living: Education and the Wealth of Nations*, (New York: Basic Books, 1992), 77.

20. Gerald Bracey, "The Propaganda of 'A Nation at Risk,'" *Education Disinformation Detection and Reporting Agency*, 15 September 1999, www.americatomorrow.com/bracey/EDDRA/EDDRA8.htm (accessed 4 November 2005).

21. Jack L. Nelson, Stuart B. Palonsky, and Mary Rose McCarthy, *Critical Issues in Education: Dialogues and Dialectics*, (Boston: McGraw-Hill, 2004), 203.

8

The Eighties and Nineties

According to the analysis of William J. Bennett, who replaced Terrell Bell as the Secretary of Education:

> In the 1960s and 1970s, we neglected and denied much of the best in American education. We simply stopped doing the right things. We allowed an assault on intellectual and moral standards. Traditional education practices were discarded, expectations were lowered, and the curriculum was "dumbed-down." . . . The effects were damaging to our well-being. We saw an alarming drop in standardized test scores, and American students suffered in virtually all international comparisons. . . . Our children were too often the victims of adults' indulgences in educational and social foolishness. . . . In reaction to this, the 1980s gave birth to a grass-roots movement for education reform that has generated a renewed commitment to excellence, character, and fundamentals.[1]

Under the leadership of Bennett, the federal education policy of the Reagan presidency has been described as the five Ds. These include "disestablishment (the elimination of the Department of Education), deregulation, decentralization, de-emphasis (the reduction of the position of education as a priority on the federal agenda), and, most importantly diminution (reduction of the Federal budget in education)."[2]

With the federal government reducing its role in the field of education, it was up to the states and local school districts to introduce the reforms being called for by the critics. The efforts initially seemed "incoherent, covering everything from increases in teachers' salaries to school finance reform to merit pay for teachers to school site-based management and internal restructuring."[3] Leaders in creating these initiatives were for the most part southern governors including Richard Riley of South Carolina, Bob Graham of Florida, and Bill Clinton of Arkansas.[4] Other reforms that began in the mid-eighties included increasing course requirements for graduation, instituting more tests, strengthening certification requirements for teachers, and in some areas lengthening the school day or year.[5]

In all of these efforts, there was little reference to the tenets of progressive education that some educational historians, at least, had all but declared dead. Lawrence Cremin pointed out that through most of the twentieth century, the primary source of unity among progressive educators had been their common "opposition to certain school practices." In Cremin's view these included criticism of the following practices in traditional schools:

- Excessive reliance on textbook methods
- Memorization of factual data and techniques by drill
- Static aims and materials that reject the notion of a changing world
- Use of fear or corporal punishment as a form of discipline
- Attempts to isolate education from child experiences and social reality[6]

For him at least, it was the failure of progressives to develop a uniform alternative to the practices that they criticized which contributed to the downfall of the movement. He also would argue that the movement failed because the progressive ideas that it advocated required highly competent teachers. It was Cremin's opinion that there were not enough of these teachers to transform our schools.[7]

During the past two decades there have been many influential critics who have written and spoken against the evils of progressive education. Calling himself a "political liberal" but an educational "conservative" or "pragmatist," author E. D. Hirsch, Jr., has claimed that progressive educational ideas have led to "failure" in our schools and "greater social inequality." For him, "the only practical way to achieve liberalism's aim of greater social justice is to pursue conservative educational policies."[8] This means that all students must be exposed to a common body of knowledge if they are to have the opportunity to succeed in our society. In his best-selling book, *Cultural Literacy,* Hirsch argues that it is especially necessary to make this common knowledge available to poor minority students. He believes that:

> The common knowledge characteristically shared by those at the top of the socioeconomic ladder in the United States should be readily available to all citizens because people who lack it suffer serious handicaps. This "core knowledge" is needed for productive communication and establishing fundamental equality as citizens. That is the content of basic education and should be the primary focus of schooling.[9]

Hirsch has gone on in later books to define an "explicit" core curriculum for all students that includes a "list of important names, dates, ideas, and allusions that all students should learn." With this curriculum, he and his colleagues have established approximately one thousand schools where this "core knowledge" is taught.[10]

Because of individuals such as Hirsch, the movement toward reform continued to gain momentum during the final years of the Reagan Administration. The new president, George H. W. Bush, was anxious to have the federal government play a more active role in education. To give focus to his education program, the Bush Administration announced its objectives in a document entitled *Goals 2000.* The six original goals were published following a meeting of the National Governors' Association in 1989. Their purpose was to set targets for education during the next decade. Included were the following:

- All children will start school ready to learn.
- High school graduation rates will be at least 90 percent.
- Students will show competence in critical subjects.
- U.S. students will be the first in the world in mathematics and science achievement.
- Every adult will be literate and have skills to compete in the economy.
- Schools will be free of drugs and violence.

During President Clinton's Administration, goals were added calling for the improvement of teacher education programs and an increase in parental involvement in schools. To attempt to reach these goals, an agency called the National Education Standards and Improvement Council was formed.[11]

This group would spearhead the effort to create national curriculum standards in the basic subjects. The hope was that by using specialists in the field, an agreement could be reached on what children should know about each academic subject at each grade level. The first of these groups to finish a set of curriculum standards was the one that had worked in the field of mathematics. Even though there was no federal mandate that states or school districts accept these national standards, in forty-one states they were used at least in part in developing state standards in mathematics education. Things did not go so well in the field of social studies, where the criticisms of the proposed standards came from all quarters. Because social studies includes not only the study of history, but also the social sciences, there were few groups who were happy with the content of the proposal in this academic area.[12]

Eventually a Republican-led Congress would decide that the effort to develop national curriculum standards was not appropriate. Along with the obvious difficulty of creating a true consensus at the national level, conservatives continued to believe that education should remain primarily a responsibility of state and local government. They did not wish to further increase the power of the federal Department of Education. As a result, every state developed its own curriculum standards for each subject. Some states turned out very specific documents that made it clear to teachers exactly what should be taught at every grade level while the curriculum standards of other states were stated as broad objectives. Those states that chose not to outline specific content at every grade level were hoping to give to individual schools and teachers a significant degree of latitude in choosing how to meet the objectives. Using this approach, it was hoped that it would allow teachers to be more creative in their teaching methods. In these states it is possible that instructors could utilize more of the methods that were supported by progressive educators.

Even with the momentum for specific curriculum standards, conservative critics of the schools remained less than satisfied with these changes. In a book titled *Educational Reform in the '90s,* the authors concluded that during the decade following the *A Nation at Risk* report, the reforms had focused primarily on "raising standards through such traditional means as stricter graduation requirements, higher teachers' salaries, and minimum competency tests for teachers and students . . . these efforts, although well-intentioned," showed little or no improvement in academic achievement.[13] As the book looked ahead, it predicted the next step in the reform movement. The authors believed that "several factors converging at the national level suggest that the federal government may in the near future no longer limit its actions to cheerleading and goal setting."[14] What they were referring to is included in the final paragraph of the book where they stress the essential nature of testing and accountability.[15] A consensus was forming among policymakers that curriculum standards were not enough to ensure increased academic achievement. President Clinton, who as governor of Arkansas had strongly supported the Goals 2000 initiative, was able to establish a more active federal role in education when he signed the *Improving America's Schools Act* in 1994.[16]

Nothing that the federal government did under President Clinton slowed the continual criticism of the public schools. Using the provocative title *Dumbing Down our Kids*, Charles J. Sykes wrote in 1995 that "America's schools are in deep trouble. Not because they lack men and women who care about children, but because they are dominated by an ideology that does not care much about learning.[17] Specifically, he includes the following arguments:

- The dumbing down of America's students is a direct result of the dumbing down of the curriculum and the standards of American schools that is the legacy of a decades-long flight from learning.
- American students are unable to effectively compete with the rest of the industrialized world because our schools teach less, expect less, and settle for less than do those of other countries.
- The decline of the reading and writing abilities of American children is directly attributable to the way those skills are—and are not—taught in American schools. American children are not learning many of the basic facts of history, geography, and science because their schools are often uninterested in teaching them.
- Even as evidence mounts that American students are lacking in basic academic skills, such as writing, reading, and mathematics, schools

are increasingly emphasizing so-called "affective" learning that deals with feelings, attitudes, and beliefs of students, rather than addressing what they know or can do.[18]

Just prior to the turn of the century, another author, Martin Gross, would write his suggestions for dealing with the perceived educational problems outlined by Sykes and others. His solutions included, among others, the following:

- To strengthen academic curriculums, students should be required to take four years of English, history, science, and mathematics. Physics, trigonometry, and intermediate algebra, along with philosophy and economics, should be part of the curriculum of every high school student.
- Teacher tenure laws should be modified to allow school boards and principals to more easily dismiss ineffective teachers.
- All undergraduate schools of education should be closed, and students should have a liberal arts degree prior to having graduate work in teacher training. Only those with at least a 3.0 grade average should be allowed into teacher education graduate programs.
- The doctorate degree called the EdD should be eliminated as it is a false doctorate.
- Teacher unions should be regulated.
- National, state, and local PTAs should be disbanded.
- Vouchers should be awarded for all children attending failing schools.
- There should be a dramatic increase in the number of alternative-teacher certification programs.
- The top-heavy school bureaucracies should be eliminated.
- Educational psychology should be eliminated from teacher education programs because they are based on a false science.
- Teacher certification tests should be made more difficult as they are presently based on the ninth or tenth grade level.[19]

All of these critics called for a return to traditional academic teaching methods. For them there was an undoubtable disdain for what they perceived as progressive education. The criticisms of the nation's schools were articulated by journalists, conservative educators, and by influential members of the business community. In the e-mail newsletter, *Capitalism Magazine,* the editor, Wayne Dunn, makes clear who he believes is responsible for the deplorable condition of the public schools. For him, the problem is "socialization," which he equates with the progressive education movement. For Mr. Dunn and many others, the villain is the so-called "education establishment" that has been indoctrinated with the ideas of John Dewey. He quotes Dewey as saying that "the mere absorbing of facts and truths, is so exclusively individual an affair that it . . . tends toward selfishness. There is no obvious social motive for . . . mere learning. There is no clear social gain."[20] For this conservative capitalist, Dewey's words are "from the poison pen of a philosopher last century . . . it's high time we toss progressive education in the dumpster."[21]

Despite the fact that criticism remained constant during the nineties, there were many who questioned its validity as well as the reforms that were being introduced. The same year as the publication of the *A Nation at Risk* report, Theodore S. Sizer, a former dean of the Harvard Graduate School of Education, wrote in his book, *Horace's Compromise,* that "machine-scored standardized tests" would not solve our educational problems. Sizer was thought by many to be the "leading voice of contemporary progressivism." His ideas combined the themes of John Dewey with "Robert Hutchin's concerns for intellectual habits and demonstrations of mastery." Sizer and his supporters put together a group of over 1,200 schools that followed his "minimalist reform ideas."[22]

Another critic of the reforms launched by the *A Nation at Risk* report is Gerald Bracey. A supporter of public schools, he became an outspoken critic of the data used in the report. In a 1991 article in the *Washington Post*, he notes that "the high school graduation rate is at an all-time high and that math scores and reading performance levels are higher than they have been for more than twenty years." He goes on to argue that schools in the United States "achieve these results despite the fact that, compared to other nations, it allots relatively fewer resources to education."[23] While admitting that our schools do have problems, Bracey was clear in expressing his opinion that "claiming that the system is failing is not only distracting, but creates the wrong climate for improvement—you don't get people to do better by telling them how lousy they are."[24] Writing twenty years after the publication of the *A Nation at Risk* report, Bracey continued to support the public schools. He has pointed out that while the schools were blamed for the poor economic times in the nation during the eighties, no one has praised the schools after the economy improved in the nineties. He goes even further by charging that some government officials "deliberately suppressed good news about the schools."[25]

Another well-known educator who has expressed reservations about the standards movement and high-stakes testing is John Goodlad. He has written that:

> Over the past year, I have been asking members of groups to which I speak to select from four items the one they believe to have the most promise for improving our schools . . .
>
> • Standards and tests mandated by all states;
> • A qualified, competent teacher in every classroom;
> • Non-promotion and grade retention for all students who fail to reach grade level standards on the tests;
> • Schools of choice for all parents.
>
> From an audience of about one thousand people at the 2001 National School Boards Association Conference, one person chose the first. All the rest chose the second, which usually is the unanimous choice, whatever the group.[26]

Jonathan Kozol also believes that teachers are the key to creating excellent schools. For him "the best teachers he knows are poets at heart who love the unpredictable aspects of teaching and the uniqueness of every child in their classes." He is convinced that these outstanding teachers are "drawn to teaching children and not to business school. Teaching to standards that are not their own will make teachers technicians, and the classroom will lose its best teachers."[27]

An outstanding school administrator from New York City, Deborah Meier, agrees that there is a crisis in education, but it is not the one described in the *A Nation at Risk* report. For her, it is the problem of providing "equity and justice for our most vulnerable citizens: the children of the poor. . . . The real crisis facing the United States is social, not academic. Children who come to school hungry and poor are not likely to be helped by more rigorous standards.[28] Today there are many educators in every state who would claim that "all too often, standards have raised the bar for students, educators, and schools, without the accompanying resources and support needed to make standards-based education work."[29]

While Sizer, Bracey, Kozol, Meier, and others have openly criticized the direction of public education in the nineties, the momentum for a major federal initiative in education continued to grow during the decade. Despite the historical position of his Republican Party concerning the role of the federal government in public education, upon taking office after his election in 1990, George W. Bush placed the need to reform our schools high on his list of legislative priorities. The opportunity came in 2002 when Title 1, the major section of the Elementary and Secondary Education Act, came before Congress for reauthorization. After months of debate and significant compromises by both parties, the result was the passage of what was called the *No Child Left Behind Act*. This legislation would attempt to use the federal government's large financial commitment to Title I as a way to force schools to accept a new accountability that had not been present in the past. It is much too early to tell whether the law will, in the long run, improve our schools. One might easily conclude that with its mandatory academic standards, high-stakes testing, and school accountability, the law will serve as the final blow to progressive education. To reach such a conclusion also may be premature. To ascertain the potential impact of the law, it is necessary to first analyze its objectives and provisions. This will be the topic of our next chapter.

NOTES

1. William J. Bennett, *Our Children and Our Country*, (New York: Simon & Schuster Inc., 1988), 9–10.

2. Kathryn M. Borman, Piyush Swami, and Lonni P. Wagstaff, eds., *Contemporary Issues in U.S. Education*, (Norwood, NJ: Ablex Publishing Corporation, 1991), 164.

3. David T. Gordon, ed., *A Nation Reformed?*, (Cambridge, MA: Harvard Education Press, 2003), 26.

4. Gordon, *A Nation Reformed?*, 26.

5. Gordon, *A Nation Reformed?*, 8.

6. Allan C. Ornstein, *Teaching and Schooling in America*, (Boston: Pearson Education Group, Inc., 2003), 319.

7. Ornstein, *Teaching and Schooling in America*, 319.

8. E. D. Hirsch, Jr., "Why Traditional Education is More Progressive," *American Enterprise Online*, March/April 1997, http://www.taemag.com/issues/articleid.16209/article_detail.asp (accessed 23 September 2005).

9. Jack L. Nelson, Stuart B. Palonsky, and Mary Rose McCarthy, *Critical Issues in Education: Dialogues and Dialectics*, (Boston: McGraw-Hill, 2004), 235.

10. Diane Ravitch, *Left Back: A Century of Battles Over School Reform*, (New York: Touchstone, 2000), 419–20.

11. Joel Spring, *American Education*, (Boston: McGraw-Hill, 1998), 22.

12. Ravitch, *Left Back: A Century of Battles Over School Reform*, 232–34.

13. Chester E. Finn, Jr., and Theodor Rebarber, eds., *Education Reforms in the '90s*, (New York: McMillan Publishing Company, 1992), vii.

14. Finn and Rebarber, *Education Reforms in the '90s*, 191.

15. Finn and Rebarber, *Education Reforms in the '90s*, 192.

16. National Conference of State Legislatures, "No Child Left Behind Act of 2001," 2004, http://www.ncsl.org/programs/educ/NCLBHistory.htm (accessed 15 March 2004), 1.

17. Charles J. Sykes, *Dumbing Down Our Kids,* (New York: St. Martin's Press, 1995), ix.

18. Sykes, *Dumbing Down Our Kids*, 9–10.

19. Martin L. Gross, *The Conspiracy of Ignorance*, (New York: Harper-Collins, 1999), 248–254.

20. *Capitalism Magazine*, "Progressive Education and Taping Kids to Dumpsters," May 3, 2004, http://capmag.com/article.asp?ID=3661 (accessed 5 July 2005), 2.

21. *Capitalism Magazine*, "Progressive Education and Taping Kids to Dumpsters," 3.

22. Ravitch, *Left Back: A Century of Battles Over School Reform*, 418.

23. Charles P. Cozic, ed., *Education in America*, (San Diego: Greenhaven Press, Inc., 1992), 25.

24. Cozic, *Education in America*, 31.

25. Don Kuchak, Paul Eggen, Mary D. Burbank, *Charting a Professional Course: Issues and Controversies in Education*, (Upper Saddle River, NJ: Pearson, 2005), 315.

26. John D. Pulliam and James Van Patten, *History of Education in America* (Englewood Cliffs, NJ: Prentice Hall, 1991), 159.

27. Nelson, Palonsky, and McCarthy, *Critical Issues in Education: Dialogues and Dialectics,* 163.

28. Nelson, Palonsky, and McCarthy, *Critical Issues in Education: Dialogues and Dialectics,* 165.

29. Nelson, Palonsky, and McCarthy, *Critical Issues in Education: Dialogues and Dialectics*, 166.

9

No Child Left Behind

By the time the presidential election campaign of 2000 was underway, it was clear that the education reforms attempted during the 1990s had yet to produce a dramatic improvement in students' test scores. The ambitious objectives established by the Goals 2000 program were allowed to lapse, and the two political parties began to search for solutions for the persistent problems plaguing schools. Some conservative Republicans were seeking to allow local and state governments additional flexibility on how to spend federal funds, especially those provided by Title I of the Elementary and Secondary Act. Other Republicans were championing a voucher system that would allow parents to send their children to either public or private schools.[1]

George W. Bush, in his 2000 presidential campaign, highlighted the issue of educational reform. As a candidate, he "took credit for the educational reform in Texas" that occurred during his governorship. Although the reforms had begun under his predecessor, Democrat Ann Richards, Governor Bush "did forcefully move" the reforms through the legislature. Despite the fact that improved test scores were "exaggerated," he was able to gain the initiative in the debate over education during the campaign. Democratic candidate Al Gore "never really found his voice on education while the Republicans advanced an ambitious reform agenda." The Republican platform supported the following:

- Private school vouchers
- Phonics-based reading programs

- Character education
- Abstinence sex education

Even though conservative Republicans were less than enthusiastic, the party also favored mandating state curriculum standards and high-stakes testing.[2]

After the election the Bush Administration moved to prepare and introduce legislation to carry out its platform. For over three decades, schools have received money from Washington for the purpose of providing remedial reading and math programs. The amount of money allotted to a school district was dependent upon the number of poor children attending that district school. The programs were carefully regulated by government officials, and most of the money was spent to hire additional remedial teachers to work with underachieving students. The impact of these appropriations was always difficult to measure, but since overall reading and math scores had failed to increase dramatically, critics believed that there must be better ways to spend the money.

The congressional debate leading up to the final passage of the No Child Left Behind legislation required many compromises. Democrats such as Ted Kennedy from Massachusetts had fought for years for a more active role by the federal government in attempting to provide an equal educational opportunity for all of the nations' children. Specifically, he wanted the federal government to provide money for schools with poor children so that these students would have the same chance to succeed educationally as children from affluent suburban homes. For most liberal Democrats, this would require a dramatic increase in federal money that could be directed to schools suffering from a lack of financial support by the state and local governments. To gain Democratic support, conservative Republicans had to agree to give more money to schools and, at least temporarily, forget about idea of a national voucher system. Even with the opposition of Democrats as well as the two national teachers' unions, the possibility of initiating some parental choice was not totally ignored in the final legislation. When the vote finally came on the law, the many compromises assured strong bipartisan support. It passed in the House of Representatives by a vote of 381 to 41 and in the Senate by a margin of 37 to 10.[3]

The nearly 2,100 pages of the law have resulted in the most all-encompassing initiative of the federal government in the field of education. Its extremely ambitious goal is to make all students and schools "proficient" by the 2013–2014 school year. Although it is impossible to summarize all of the sections of the law, there are several significant provisions that are likely to have the most impact on our schools. They would include the following:

- Schools, districts, and states must show Adequate Yearly Progress as measured by tests that are designed to determine a student's knowledge of curriculum standards that must be developed in every state. These curriculum standards would be created for every major academic area. The test results must demonstrate student progress by the entire student body as well as progress by specific groups whose scores would be "disaggregated." The groups which will be separated out would include the following:

  1. Economically disadvantaged students
  2. Major racial and ethnic groups
  3. Students with disabilities
  4. English language learners (ELL)[4]

- All of the information concerning students' test scores, as well as information concerning all teachers in the school districts, must be reported to the public annually. This "report card" will be published along with comparisons with other districts. The obvious purpose of this reporting mandate is to make all schools accountable to their communities.[5]

- Timelines are established in the law for schools whose test scores classify them as "schools in need of improvement." These "low-performing" or "failing" schools must take corrective action. These corrective actions include:

  1. Schools that fail to meet "Adequate Yearly Progress" (AYP), for two consecutive years, must be identified as "needing improvement."
  2. Schools that fail to meet the state AYP standards for three consecutive years must offer pupils from low-income families the

opportunity to receive instruction from a supplemental services provider of the parents' choice. This could include for-profit tutoring companies.

3. Schools that fail to meet AYP for four consecutive years must take one or more of the following corrective actions: replace school staff, implement a new curriculum, decrease management authority, appoint an outside expert to advise the school, extend the school day or year, or change the school's internal organization structure.

4. Schools that fail to meet AYP standards for five consecutive years must be restructured, which includes reopening as a charter school, replacing all or most school staff, state takeover of school operations, or other "major restructuring" of school governance.[6]

• The law emphasizes a stronger commitment to reading education, especially with our youngest children. A new Reading First grant program is included in the legislation. School districts that are successful in gaining one of these grants will use the money to assist children in grades K–3 who are at risk of reading failure. The grants also provide professional development opportunities in the field of reading instruction for teachers of grades K–3.

• There is also a new grant program for states to improve teacher quality. These grants focus on providing assistance to schools in utilizing "scientifically based research to prepare, train, and recruit high-quality teachers."

• The law also makes available assistance to state and local districts that are seeking to provide safe, drug-free schools. States must allow students who attend a persistently dangerous school or who are victims of violent crimes at school, to transfer to a safe school.[7]

One final section of the law deals with the mandate that schools have only "highly qualified teachers." The original legislation sets the 2005–2006 school year as the time limit for school districts to ensure that "all teachers of core academic subjects be highly qualified." This has been determined to mean that they should be "fully licensed or certified by the state" in which they teach. For elementary teachers, a bachelor's degree is the minimum academic requirement along with the passing of a rigorous test that covers all areas of the curriculum. Middle school and high school teachers would need to pass a "rigorous test in the subject areas they were teaching."[8] This provision of the law, like a number of others, has been modified and the deadline for compliance has been extended. School districts will now have one additional year, which will be granted "contingent on evidence that a state had been reordering its priorities and building the systems needed to take responsibility for the quality of its teaching force under the *No Child Left Behind Act*. The deal also requires a state to map out how it intends to move forward and then subject that map to the scrutiny of federal officials."[9]

The above provisions are merely the highlights of the hundreds and hundreds of pages of the legislation. Despite the complexity, the Bush Administration was able to convince large majorities in both houses of Congress to support the law. In the weeks following its passage, there was generally a positive reaction to this new federal initiative in the field of public education. As states and school districts began to become familiar with the specifics of the law and with the administrative guidelines that were prepared to carry out the legislation, serious opposition emerged. Complaints began to come not only from state officials but also from individual school districts. As the 2004 presidential election campaign began to heat up, Senator Kennedy, as well as other Democrats who had voted for the law, began to criticize President Bush for failing to provide the promised funding. While campaigning for his fellow Massachusetts senator, John Kerry, Senator Kennedy stated that Congress had authorized 18.5 billion dollars for Title I, but the budget President Bush sent to Congress included only 12.35 billion. He went on to say that "President Bush thinks he is providing enough for schools. Parents, teachers, and I don't."[10]

Not only was there criticism by members of Congress, but there were serious legal challenges to provisions of the law by state legislatures, teacher unions, such as the National Education Association, and from individual districts. As school opened in September of 2005, forty-seven of the fifty states were in some "stage of rebellion" against sections of the law. In twenty states there has been at least discussion of opting out of some or all of the requirements, even if it means foregoing the federal funding available under Title I of the Elementary and Secondary Act. This money, of course, is the way the Department of Education expects to force compliance with the law. The state of Connecticut has filed a major lawsuit claiming that the federal aid being made available is insufficient for financing the cost of meeting the new mandates.[11] In addition to Connecticut's challenge, the state legislature in Utah has notified the federal Department of Education that their state will not enforce any aspects of the law that are contrary to the current educational policies and objectives of their state. Even President Bush's own state of Texas has been refusing to carry out several mandates and has been fined more than $440,000 for missing data-reporting deadlines. Among other problems, the state has decided to disregard the No Child Left Behind requirement for testing students with learning disabilities.[12]

With the legislation up for review in 2007, it appears likely that there will be ongoing conflict as the federal Department of Education attempts to effectively administer the law. In response to the many criticisms, Secretary of Education Margaret Spelling has made compromises on a number of enforcement issues. Along with the extension available to districts for having only "highly qualified" teachers, there have been changes in the regulations concerning reporting procedures, especially in regard to special education children.

Because of the ever-increasing federal deficit, the issue of adequately financing the law continues to plague the Bush Administration. The *New York Times* in July of 2005 contained a story claiming that funding for low-income students was being reduced in the federal budget. Despite the overall increase in Title I spending, the paper reports that funds for high-poverty districts will decline by 3.2 percent in the coming year. The analysis done by the Center on Education Policy gives new data to critics in pursuing the argument that the Bush Administration is not really serious about meeting the objectives of the law.[13]

Among the many critics of the law since its passage are several who consider themselves progressive educators. Harold Berlak, a self-described "progressive educator," believes that "progressive educators aim to engage the learner, nurture imagination, cognitive and artistic expression, and foster social-emotional and moral development." For him, progressive education is about "student centered" learning and concern for the "whole child." Needless to say, this philosophy is consistent with what John Dewey was writing a century ago. For Mr. Berlak, the most disturbing aspect of the No Child Left Behind initiative is that "all curriculum materials and services for teaching reading (and soon math) must be approved in advance as scientifically based." This approach, he believes, will "censor curriculum materials" and teaching methods that "don't fit the government's pro-corporate, right-wing education agenda."[14]

To deal with the current realities, Berlak calls for a "new unified progressive education movement" that would reassert "the fundamental political and pedagogical values of progressive education." Such a movement must convince the public that progressive education has not been a historic failure. This point of view, he suggests, has been accepted by a significant number of Americans.[15]

Although many Americans are confused about the initiatives contained in the No Child Left Behind legislation, most are probably aware that it is emphasizing a traditional, back-to-basics approach. The specific curriculum standards for every subject at every grade level, along with the high-stakes testing, have undoubtedly created a realization among parents that these tests are important. Many believe that teachers are feeling the pressure to "teach to the test." In a publication of the Institute for America's Future, Earl Hadley has written about the way the law is being enforced. He objects to using threats of withholding funds and firing teachers whose test scores are low as this only leads to a "focus on testing—not learning. In a best-case scenario, this means a shrinking of the curriculum toward tested subjects." For the immediate future, that would mean any subjects except language arts, mathematics, or science. "At their worst, these pressures can lead to teachers cheating to improve test scores."[16] Still others complain about the added strain on students caused by the tests.

It is not surprising that many of those who are finding fault with the current initiatives would be those who would support an approach more in keeping with progressive education. Yet, given the demands for improving test scores, one could question whether or not there will be sufficient pressure to create another historic shift in the way Americans think about their schools. Or perhaps by asking the question in a different way, one might wonder if we have indeed seen the final demise of what we call progressive education. It is difficult to know as we begin a new century whether the No Child Left Behind law will result in the end of any influence over our schools by John Dewey and the other progressive leaders. The other possibility is that there will once again be a renewal of these ideas as people become disenchanted with our current reform movement.

The remainder of this book will be devoted to this question. We will begin by examining a relic of the early progressive movement that appears to be continuing to prosper in the United States. Today, thousands of parents are choosing to send their young children to what are now called Montessori Schools. It is possible that the popularity of this approach to learning is an indication that there remains a strong market for progressivism in education in our country. In the next chapter, we will examine the Montessori movement and whether it might become even more significant in the twenty-first century.

NOTES

1. David T. Gordon, ed., *A Nation Reformed?*, (Cambridge, MA: Harvard Education Press, 2003), 126–27.

2. L. Dean Webb, *The History of American Education*, (Upper Saddle River, NJ: Pearson, 2006), 360.

3. National Conference of State Legislatures, "No Child Left Behind Act of 2001," http://www.ncsl.org/programs/educ/NCLBHistory.htm (accessed 15 March 2004), 1.

4. James A. Johnson, Diann Musial, Gene E. Hall, Donna M. Gollnick, and Victor L. Dupuis, *Foundations of American Education*, (Boston: Pearson, 2005), 137.

5. "No Child Left Behind," *Education Week*, at www.edweek.org/context/topics/issuepage.cfm?id=59 (accessed 14 September 2004), 1–3.

6. Johnson, Musial, Hall, Gollnick, and Dupuis, *Foundations of American Education*, 158.

7. U.S. Department of Education, "Executive Summary," January 2001, http://www.ed.gov/nclb/overview/intro/excusumm.html?exp=0 (accessed 19 March 2004), 1.

8. Johnson, Musial, Hall, Gollnick, and Dupuis, *Foundations of American Education*, 157.

9. "States Given Extra Year on Teachers," *Education Week* at http://www.edweek.org/ew/articles/2005/11/02/10reprieve.h25.html?rale=KQE5d7nM%2..., (accessed 4 November 2005), 1.

10. CNN.com, "Bush Makes Money, Touts Education," *Inside Politics*, 6 January 2004, http://www.cnn.com/2004/ALLPOLITICS/01/06/elec04.prezbush.fundraising.ap/(accessed 6 January 2004), 1–2.

11. "Bush Faces Growing Revolt Over Educational Policy," *Public News Room* at http://www.publicbroadcasting.net/kplu/newsmain?action=article& ARTICLE-ID (accessed 2 September 2005), 1.

12. Kavan Peterson, *"No Letup in Unrest Over Bush School Law," Stateline.org* at http://www.stateline.org/View Page.action?siteNodeId=136&language Id=1&contentId=... (accessed 4 August 2005), 1–2.

13. Michael Janofski, "Federal Spending Increases, but More Schools Will Get Less Money for Low-Income Students," *New York Times*, 4 July 2005, A9.

14. Harold Berlak, "Education Policy 1964–2004: The *No Child Left Behind* and the Assault on Progressive Education and Local Control," http://www.pipeline .com/~rougeforum/PolicyandNCLB.htm (accessed 17 March 2005), 1, 5.

15. Berlak, "Education Policy 1964–2004: The *No Child Left Behind* and the Assault on Progressive Education and Local Control," 5–6.

16. Earl Hadley, "A Progressive Education," http://www.tompaine.com/articles/ 20050503/a_progressive_education.php (accessed 5 July 2005), 2.

10

Maria Montessori

Maria Montessori (1870–1952) was a contemporary of John Dewey (1859–1952), but their life stories are quite different. Dewey was very much an academic, who with the exception of his work with the Laboratory School at the University of Chicago, spent his professional life as a college professor and author. Maria Montessori had a much different career pattern. Although they were dissimilar in many ways, their impact on American education in the twentieth century places them both in a prominent position in the history of the progressive education movement.

Born only ten years after the Italian Unification, Maria was raised in a society that was very traditional and conservative. Women were expected to be "the central sustaining force in their families." Their educational opportunities were greatly restricted, even though as a member of the middle class, Maria was given the opportunity to at least complete elementary school. She was unique in that at an early age she was determined to continue her education in a secondary school and to eventually enter medical school. Even as a young student, Maria reacted against the teacher-centered instruction methods prevalent in the schools she attended. In these classrooms "children stood when questioned by the teacher and provided accurately memorized responses from the textbook. Italian schools, in particular, featured dictation, in which students would copy word for word statements made by the teacher."[1] Maria Montessori would spend her adult life attempting to provide methods of teaching and learning that would improve upon this model.

Following her years in the secondary school, she was the first woman accepted into an Italian medical school. Her own father did not approve of what was, in his mind, an "outrageous" career choice for a woman. Acceptance into the program itself did not guarantee an equal educational opportunity for Maria. She was not allowed to participate in dissecting activities with the male students and was forced to enter the laboratory late at night to complete her assignments. Even with these restrictions, her work as a student was exceptional enough that she was awarded annual scholarships by the university. Graduating in 1896, Maria accepted the position as the assistant doctor at the psychiatric clinic of the University of Rome. In this capacity, she spent much of her time working with mentally disabled children. This experience caused her to conclude that "retardation should be treated as a pedagogical, rather than a medical, problem." To test this idea, she created "the first orthrophrenic school in Rome to work specifically with exceptional children." Her approach for working with these special children established her as an educational expert in the city of Rome. As a result, she was in demand as a speaker, and she became a lecturer in educational methods at the University of Rome. Even her father came to be proud of her accomplishments and growing reputation. On her thirtieth birthday he presented her with an album containing two hundred newspaper articles about her work.[2]

Her reputation continued to grow as the students in her school began to show dramatic educational progress. This was demonstrated as the majority of her students were able to pass the state-sponsored examinations. After observing the success of her methods, with what we would call today special education students, she began to think about using the same approach with "normal children." With this in mind, Maria established her first Casa dei Bambini (Children's house) in 1907. Her work would be recognized for the achievement of the students and for Maria's unique approach to education. She soon would become well-known not only in Europe but also in the United States. By 1915, there were already one hundred schools here utilizing her methods. Jean Piaget (1896–1980) was a director of "the modified Montessori school" in Geneva, Switzerland. While working in the school, he observed closely the Montessori approach and wrote favorably about it in his first book, *Language and Thought of the Child*. His commitment to the methods advocated by Maria Montessori led him to become the head of the Swiss Montessori Society.[3]

Maria Montessori's prominence in the United States was enhanced by a visit here in 1915. Invited by Alexander Graham Bell, Thomas Edison, and others, she spoke at Carnegie Hall. Later in her trip, she set up a model classroom at the Panama-Pacific Exposition in San Francisco. Thousands of visitors were able to observe this functioning classroom where a teacher and twenty-one students demonstrated the Montessori methods.

After World War I, the popularity of the Montessori methods in the United States rapidly declined. This was "partly due to her insistence that only she could train teachers in her method and that only she should control the manufacture and distribution of her teaching materials."[4] There had also been a book published in 1914 by John Dewey's disciple William Heard Kilpatrick that denounced the Montessori method as "out of date."

In 1934, Mussolini's fascist government closed all of the Montessori schools in Italy. Because of her antifascist views, Maria was exiled from Italy. She spent the years during and immediately following the war spreading her ideas throughout the world.[5] Living primarily in India, she was known not only as an educator but as a crusader for a more peaceful world. On three separate occasions, she was nominated for the Nobel Peace Prize.[6] It was not until 1949 that she was welcomed back to her homeland, where she lived just three years longer.[7]

Even after her death, there were scattered Montessori programs in many countries, including the United States, but the most rapid growth has occurred since 1990.[8] Although it is difficult to know precisely, it is now estimated that there are more than five thousand Montessori schools in the United States.[9] All but a few hundred of these programs are privately run, although there have been a number that have been created as part of public school choice programs. Montessori classes most frequently place children in three-year age groups (3–6, 6–9, 9–12). By far the most popular are the classes for the younger age group. Because the vast majority of the schools are private, parents are required to pay tuition. Tuition at Montessori schools ranges from a low of under $1,000 per year to a high of over $11,000 per year. One estimate placed the median annual tuition for the youngest age group at $3,400 per year.[10]

To operate a certified Montessori school or classroom, teachers must have special training. Although anyone can use the name "Montessori" in describing a training program, the two major organizations providing instruction for the Montessori method are the Association Montessori International and the American Montessori Society. Most training centers mandate that candidates have a bachelor's degree prior to admission. It is also possible for teachers to be trained online, although such training might not lead to employment in a certified Montessori school.[11]

Through the years many famous people have been associated with Montessori schools in one way or another. The list includes Julia Child, Helen Keller, Alexander Graham Bell, Thomas Edison, Henry Ford, Mahatma Gandhi, Sigmund Freud, Leo Tolstoy, the Dalai Lama, Jacqueline Kennedy, Prince William and Prince Harry of the English royal family, Bill and Hillary Clinton, and Yo-Yo Ma. Three well-known successful American entrepreneurs who credit their Montessori training are Jeff Bezos of Amazon.com and Larry Page and Sergey Brin, the founders of Google.[12]

Despite the fact that her theories have had an uneven history during the twentieth century, the ideas of Maria Montessori appear to be more popular than ever in the United States. To understand the relationship of these ideas and those of other progressives, one might consider the following summary, which appears in a teacher education textbook:

> Montessori believed that respect for children was the cornerstone on which all approaches to teaching should rest. She thought that because each child is unique, education should be individualized for each child. She also maintained that children are not miniature adults and should not be treated as such. Furthermore, Montessori believed that children are not educated by others, but rather educate themselves. To help them achieve this self-education, she recommended a prepared environment in which children could do things for themselves. Regarding the role of the teacher, Montessori believed teachers should make children the center of learning, encourage children to learn through the freedom provided in the prepared environment, and be keen observers in order to plan appropriately for children's learning.[13]

As mentioned earlier, some of Dewey's disciples were critical of aspects of the Montessori approach. Dewey himself, in his book *Democracy and Education*, takes issue with what he considers "prestructuring" of experiences and materials. For Dewey, the primary fallacy in Montessori's techniques was that they "are so anxious to get at intellectual distinctions, without waste of time, that they tend to ignore—or reduce—the immediate crude handling of the familiar material of experience, and to introduce pupils at once to the material. For Dewey at least "the first stage of contact with any new material, at whatever age or maturity, must inevitably be of the trial and error sort."[14]

He believed that a problem in the Montessori method was that it tended to suppose that we can begin with the ready-made subject matter of arithmetic, or geography, or whatever, irrespective of some direct experience of a situation. In other words, Dewey believed that the experiences created in the Montessori classroom were too structured and that it was better for students to learn by trial and error.

While Dewey would have students come upon a problem and use the scientific method to solve it, Montessori would have a preconceived plan for the students. She believed that they were "innately self-motivated" and it was the teacher's job to provide appropriate sensory motor activities. Her prepared lessons were built on this insight and might well engage all of the students' five senses and require them to manipulate various objects. An illustration would be the use of sandpaper letters designed to be touched that would be part of lessons to teach the alphabet. Preschoolers might be given cylinder blocks to help build "fine motor, analytical, and comparative language skills." A child in fourth grade might be allowed to work with interactive maps in learning about geography.[15] Lessons would also include "real-world" experiences such as washing dishes. "Manners, respect, and a sense of community are emphasized." Despite the somewhat structured nature of the classroom, there still is great flexibility in that learning is for the most part "self-directed" with the students choosing "their work each day from available lessons." "Teachers guide the process and ensure that all academic bases are covered, but the student defines her own pace and timing."[16] In this way, her thinking would be in line with John Dewey and other progressive educators.

Dewey and Montessori would also agree that schools should place a high priority on fostering the curiosity and creativity of children. Both would be critical of "mindless memorization" and would instead seek to develop students to "become self-confident, independent thinkers who learn because they are interested in the world and are enthusiastic about life." It was essential to each of them that students be interested in much more than earning good grades.[17]

Both of these educational pioneers would support the idea of a classroom as a community of learners whose members respect each other. Dewey and other early progressives would also applaud the group work and projects that were an important part of the Montessori approach. In addition, helping students to discover information for themselves in an atmosphere where there is freedom of movement and a flexible schedule would also be a common thread in the thinking of both Montessori and Dewey. If one were to look at any progressive education classroom, it would be hoped that it would be "bright, warm, and inviting, filled with plants, animals, art, music, and books." Today there might well be interest centers for each subject that would offer children "intriguing learning materials, fascinating mathematical models, maps, charts, fossils, historical artifacts, computers, scientific apparatus, perhaps a small natural-science museum, and animals that the children are raising."[18] It would also be hard to imagine any progressive educator in any era who would not support these following goals that are taught to Montessori teachers:

- to awaken the spirit and the imagination;
- to encourage the child's normal desire for independence and self-esteem;
- to help him develop the kindness, courtesy, and self-discipline that will allow him to become a contributing member of society; and
- to help the child learn how to observe, question, and explore ideas independently.[19]

Like other progressive educators, Montessori teachers are trained to pay attention to "delineation of a scale of sensitive periods of development, which provide a focus for class work that is appropriate and uniquely stimulating and motivating to the child (including sensitive periods for language development, sensorial experimentation and refinement, and various levels of social interaction)."[20] Montessori required that teachers in her schools be given specific training in what she called the "science of observation." She believed it was possible to observe "the mental development of children as natural phenomena and under experimental conditions." This allowed a school to become "a type of scientific environment devoted to the psychogenetic study of man."[21] Again, Dewey and other progressives also thought of education in terms of science.

Even with the differences between Montessori and some other progressive educators, there is little question that the philosophies and goals of all of these individuals were contrary to a system of teacher-centered learning. More important, in regard to the purposes of this study, it seems clear that in the United States, Montessori schools are an example of the continuing impact of progressive education ideas. Although the Montessori approach is well-known throughout the nation, there are other examples of progressive education in the United States.

In 1919, Rudolf Steiner founded the Waldorf School in Stuttgart, Germany. Like the Montessori schools, the Waldorf system is also expanding rapidly in communities throughout the world. The similarities between the two systems include:

- Both emphasize the education of the whole child—spiritual, mental, physical, psychological—over any particular academic curriculum.
- Both stress the importance of the natural environment, keeping in touch with nature, and natural materials.
- Both systems base their education on the needs of the child, believing that this will lead to meeting the needs of society as a whole.
- Both schools provide a rich variety of art, music, dance, and theater, at all ages.[22]

Perhaps the biggest difference is that "academic subjects are kept from children in Waldorf schools until a much later age than Montessori." For young children in these schools, the day is filled with make-believe, art, and music. Reading, writing, and math would begin sometime around age seven. These classes would be held with children their own age rather than the mixed-age groups used in the Montessori system. In the Waldorf system, the progressive approaches to learning are for the most part confined to young children.[23]

In any case, it appears evident that at least in these two educational approaches, many of the ideas of the early progressives are alive and at least for now, prospering. On the other hand, they are primarily confined to private schools where parents pay tuition. As a result, with the exception of a few hundred publicly supported Montessori schools in the United States, the children in these classrooms are most often not poor children. It is also true that the vast majority are most likely white children as opposed to the growing number of nonwhite students in our public schools. That is not to say that the ideas of Maria Montessori and Rudolph Steiner have not influenced publicly supported programs, such as Head Start. It is also true that public programs for younger children have frequently used the same techniques used in private schools. The greatest influence has been at the preschool level, but even many public elementary schools have attempted to create classroom environments similar to those advocated by Maria Montessori.

An important question regarding the future is to try to ascertain how the progressive ideas of Maria Montessori and others will be affected by the No Child Left Behind legislation. Certainly the mandated tests beginning at the third-grade level will affect how and what teachers do in their classrooms. One can only wonder if the children and parents who are currently being exposed to progressive educational approaches in preschool and kindergarten programs will balk at a more rigid classroom environment that emphasizes preparing for standardized tests. Another possibility is that the need for improving test results will pressure preschool and kindergarten through second-grade teachers to adopt more traditional teaching methods. If this begins to happen, the educational pendulum will move even further toward traditional teacher-centered approaches to education.

While it is possible that during the next few years the move toward more conservative methods in our schools will accelerate, there are reasons to guess that this might not happen. One factor that is keeping alive the ideas of Dewey and Montessori is the current curriculum of most teacher-training institutions. In these programs one can find numerous examples suggesting that, at least in teacher education courses, progressive education is very much alive. The purpose of the next chapter will be to consider the impact of teacher education programs on what is actually happening in our schools.

NOTES

1. Gerald L. Gutek, *Historical and Philosophical Foundations of Education*, (Upper Saddle River, NJ: Pearson, 2005), 355–56.
2. Madonna M. Murphy, *The History and Philosophy of Education*, (Upper Saddle River, NJ: Pearson, 2006), 368.

3. Marsha Familaro Enright and Doris Cox, "Foundations Study Guide: Montessori Education," The Objectivist Center, at http://www.objectivistcenter .org/articles/foundations_montessori-education.asp. (accessed 16 November 2005), 2.

4. "The Montessori Movement," at http://www.everything2.com/index .pl?node_id=1698329 (accessed 30 September 2005), 2.

5. "Dr. Maria Montessori," at http://www.montessori.edu/maria.html (accessed 8 July 2005), 1–2.

6. "The Montessori Movement," 2.

7. "The Montessori Movement," 2.

8. John D. Pulliam and James J. VanPatten, *History of Education in America*, (Upper Saddle River, NJ: Merrill, 1999), 151.

9. Sierra Montessori Academy, "Montessori Educational Philosophy," at http://www.sierramontessori.org/EducationalPhilosophy.htm (accessed 16 November 2005), 1.

10. "Montessori FAQ's," at http://www.michaelolaf.net/FAQMontessori.html (accessed 16 November 2005), 1.

11. "Montessori FAQ's," 3.

12. "Montessori Supporters," at http://wwwmichaelolaf.net/google.html (accessed 16 November 2005), 1.

13. George S. Morrison, *Teaching in America*, (Boston: Pearson & AB, 2006), 332.

14. John Dewey, *Democracy and Education*, (New York: The Free Press, 1916), 153–54.

15. Hobey, "The Montessori Story," Chicago Parent, at http://www.chicago parent.com/mainasp?SectionID=9&SubSectionID=29&ArticleID=59... (accessed 16 November 2005), 2.

16. Hobey, "The Montessori Story," 3.

17. Sierra Montessori Academy, "Montessori Educational Philosophy," 1.

18. Sierra Montessori Academy, "Montessori Educational Philosophy," 3.

19. Sierra Montessori Academy, "Montessori Educational Philosophy," 6.

20. "Maria Montessori," http://en.wikipedia.org/wiki/Maria_Montessori (accessed 8 July 2005), 1.

21. Herman Rohrs, *PROSPECT: The Quarterly Review of Comparative Education*, "Maria Montessori," (Paris: UNESCO, 2000), 174–175.

22. Susan Mayclin Stephenson, "Montessori and Waldorf Schools," at http:// www.michaelolaf.net/MONTESSORI%20and%20WALDORF.html (accessed 16 November 2005), 1.

23. Stephenson, "Montessori and Waldorf Schools," 1.

11

Teacher Education Programs

For most of the last century, traditional educators have been critical of teacher education programs. Whether it be the normal schools, first established by Horace Mann, or the current programs being used to train teachers, there have been ongoing attacks on the curricula designed to prepare teachers. Typical of the criticisms would be these sentiments contained in a 1956 book by Kenneth Hansen, who wrote:

> There is a common belief today, expressed quite often by some members of the faculties of our colleges and universities and rather frequently by self-appointed spokesmen for the general public, that teacher education is a pretty sorry affair. Even among students who are engaged in taking such a program, or teachers who have completed it, it is not unknown to hear complaints about the dullness, overlapping, repetitiousness, and the impractical approach of "education" courses. The professors of education and the textbooks in education are subject to the same criticisms.[1]

Specifically, it has frequently been the charge that college departments of teacher education are peddling liberal progressive education theories and that the result has been lower student achievement in the schools. For example, Robert Gray Holland, a journalist, suggested in a 1994 book titled *To Build a Better Teacher* that education professors in their "ivory towers" believe that teachers should be "facilitators of learning rather than transmitters of knowledge." He points to a 1997 study that suggests that professors are at odds with the thinking of the general public who want their children "to acquire basic knowledge and skills, in orderly and well-disciplined classrooms." The disconnect he argues, is evident in the study that found that 79 percent of education professors believe that the views of the public on education are "outmoded and mistaken."[2]

In his review of David F. Labaree's *The Trouble with Ed Schools*, Nathan Glazer refers to such writers as James Koerner in the 1960s and to E. D. Hirsch, Diane Ravitch, and Chester Finn who more recently have blamed schools of education for contributing to the "poor results in American schools." For these critics, progressive education theory has become embroiled in the culture of the schools of education. The trouble with education schools, according to Larabee, is that John Dewey's pedagogical and curriculum approach shapes "what teachers are taught, and what professors of education prefer."[3]

The conflict over what should be the appropriate preparation for teachers has continued into the twenty-first century, although a consensus on the general makeup of the curriculum has been accepted. For most teacher preparation programs, it has been agreed that all teachers should have some background in all of the liberal arts. In addition, there has been increasing pressure that teachers, especially at the secondary level, have a strong major in the areas that they will teach. For example, English teachers need to devote a large portion of their time in college to the study of literature, composition, and other communication courses. Along with their liberal arts and area of academic concentration, future teachers are required to take a number of classes in the education department. The courses include such things as child development, methods of teaching, and classroom management. As part of these classes and other education classes, students are given an increasing amount of time to observe and participate in classrooms that contain the level of students they are preparing to teach. The problem lies in determining the right balance for these three types of courses. At one extreme, there are those who feel that learning about the profession and how to teach should be the primary goal of the program, while there are others at the same college who see little value in education classes. These professors believe that the biggest problem with the preparation of future teachers is that they are not adequately prepared in the liberal arts and in the subject areas they are teaching.

One of the related issues that we have continued to debate for a half century is whether or not teachers should first obtain a liberal arts education with an academic major and then seek a masters degree in the field of education. Such an approach was suggested in the report *The Education of American Teachers*, written by James B. Conant in 1963.[4] A number of universities have created graduate education programs for those who have completed their bachelors degree in other fields. The fact is that currently the so-called "career changer" programs are preparing a significant percentage of those entering the teaching profession. Many of these individuals have completed degrees in a variety of subjects and have spent years in other careers. They have either lost their jobs or have decided that teaching would be a more rewarding career. Others are parents, who after graduating with a bachelors degree, took time off to raise their children and are now looking to begin a career. While the number of future teachers being prepared as part of a graduate program continues to grow, the majority of our future teachers are still graduating from bachelor degree programs in which they are considered teacher education majors.

There are two primary varieties of such programs. Some colleges use the first two years of a student's college education to provide a liberal arts background. This is done prior to having students officially enter the education portion of their program. The other approach is to intersperse education courses with liberal arts classes beginning in the freshman year. This pattern allows students to experience real elementary and secondary classrooms throughout their bachelors degree program. These experiences can help students to better make a realistic decision as to whether teaching is the right job for them. In any case, there is a growing agreement that these classroom observation and participation opportunities are crucial to all teacher education programs. This idea is reinforced as the hours mandated for these experiences are enforced by state and accrediting bodies. Whatever approach a college decides upon, a significant number of weeks is also set aside near the end of the program for an extensive student teaching or internship experience. Although the debate continues in every college over the appropriate breakdown between courses involving liberal arts, an academic major, and education courses, it is also an open question as to whether the teacher education offerings are a haven for progressive education theory.

In order to answer the question as to whether teacher education programs will contribute to keeping alive the theories associated with progressive education, it is helpful to survey the textbooks and syllabi of teacher education classes. Almost all future teachers, whether they take their education courses at the graduate or undergraduate level, will take a class entitled either Foundations of Education or Introduction to Education. This course is often the first class in the program and it provides a survey of many topics related to education. One of the subjects that is almost always included in the textbooks for this course is the history of education. Without exception, these historical accounts include sections dealing with progressive educators and their educational theories. Most prominent in these sections of the textbook are descriptions of the influence of John Dewey, Maria Montessori, and others. Thus, the first-year education student, early in his or her program, will undoubtedly learn something about the historical influence of progressive education along with being exposed to a summary of its major tenets.

These segments of the textbooks do not refer to John Dewey as a relic of the past but rather a continuing influence on American education. Typical would be these words found in a popular Foundations of Education textbook:

> Today, Dewey's writings and ideas continue to motivate and intrigue educators, and there still exists educational monuments to Dewey, both in a variety of school practices and in professional organizations. . . . Dewey's philosophy helped open schools to innovation and integrated education with the outside world.[5]

Along with chapters on the history of education, such textbooks also contain sections dealing with educational philosophy and theory. Once again, the writings of American progressive educators are featured. For example, in the chapter on educational philosophy, in the ninth edition of a text entitled *Foundations of Education* by Allan C. Orsntein and Daniel U. Levine, the authors have written about pragmatism and summarized John Dewey's approach as follows:

> Dewey stressed the process of problem solving. For Dewey, learning occurs as the person engages in problem solving. In this experimental epistemology, the learner, as an individual or as a member of a group, uses the scientific method to solve both personal and social problems. For Dewey, the problem solving method can be developed into a habit that transfers to a wide variety of situations.[6]

In addition to the portions of the book relating to history and philosophy, many of the foundations texts include numerous sections relating to topics that have been highlighted in the literature of the progressive educators. Chapters on student diversity highlight concepts, such as differing learning styles, multiple and emotional intelligence, special education, and gifted and talented education. These segments of the text invariably urge students to use a variety of teaching techniques in order to meet the needs of their diverse classes. Even in their initial education class, they hear about the project method of teaching, cooperative learning, simulations, and student debates.

Following their introductory class, elementary teacher education students are exposed to a variety of courses in the methods of teaching. These courses might include a separate methods class in each of the major academic subjects. For example, these students might take individual classes in the areas of language arts, mathematics, science, and social studies. Because of its importance, these same students might take one or more courses in reading education. At the secondary level, there will undoubtedly be a major class on how to teach their specific academic discipline. It is in these methods classes that students are introduced to a wide variety of teaching approaches. Many of these methods go far beyond what traditional instructors might consider for their classes. It would seem that the authors of most methods books would agree with these words written by Horace Mann many years ago. He believed that teachers must have:

> a knowledge of methods and processes. These are indefinitely various . . .
> he who is apt to teach is acquainted, not only with the common methods for
> common minds but with peculiar methods for pupils of peculiar dispositions
> and temperaments; and he is acquainted with the principles of all methods,
> whereby he can vary his plan, according to any differences in circum-
> stances.[7]

It goes without saying that methods textbooks would be very thin if they concentrated on only the traditional approach of teachers as communicators of knowledge. It is true that in introducing teacher education students to a variety of approaches, they are following at least in part, the theories of progressive educators.

Early in their training, college students are also introduced to the category known as special education. Since the 1975 passage of the Individuals with Disabilities Education Act, American schools have been mandated to provide an appropriate education to all children. Students with specific learning problems are entitled to have an individual education plan (IEP). In addition, whatever their educational liability, they must be placed in the "least restrictive environment." Currently this means that of the approximately 11 percent of American children who have been identified as being in need of special education, a large percentage will placed in regular classrooms. As a result, teachers must be prepared to work with students who have previously been in self-contained special education classes. Children who are mentally, physically, or emotionally disabled are in the same class with children without these disabilities. In one class, an instructor might have a student with an IQ below 70 sitting next to a child who has scored 140 on the same test. These so-called "inclusion" classes require that teachers find ways to meet the needs of these very different students. Especially at the elementary level, schools are seeking teacher candidates with extensive special education training. For these schools, candidates with dual certification in the elementary and special education fields are highly prized. College classes in special education even more than general education classes emphasize the importance of teaching individuals and not classes.

On the other side of the spectrum, education programs also highlight an area known as gifted and talented education. Here too, the goal is to provide special educational opportunities for those students who are judged to be intellectually superior to their classmates. With these students, traditional teaching methods geared for children with average intellectual skills may be boring and create a sense of frustration. As a result, many schools have sought ways to provide more in-depth experiences for gifted students that will challenge them intellectually. Frequently, teachers responsible for such students are urged to assign special projects that will excite them and allow them to enrich their education. Such an approach is definitely consistent with the theory that is advanced by progressive educators.

Today the concept known as multicultural education is also calling for variety in educational programs. As part of this concept, there is the theory that learning styles are affected by one's cultural background. Future teachers are being taught that the language and culture of African-American students should be considered as they plan their instruction. Even the gender of students should not be ignored in planning lessons as texts cite studies showing that girls' learning styles differ from those of boys.

While being asked to take into account all of these many differences among students, future teachers are also taught the importance of engaging students as a means for maintaining a well-managed classroom. Any book or instructor teaching classroom management skills would emphasize the fact that in order to avoid discipline problems, teachers must provide their students with activities that will engage them and thus keep their attention. In an age where students are subject daily to the rapid pace of television and computer games, keeping students involved in learning for an extended period of time is a challenge. Of course it is when students are disinterested in their classwork that misbehavior is most likely to occur. This problem has been made even more challenging by the recent trend known as block scheduling, which creates substantially longer classes. Especially with extended class periods, education professors strongly recommend that each class include a variety of activities. Thus, a typical lesson plan might have a segment where the teacher is making a presentation, and this would be followed by some sort of group activity or individual project.

At the elementary level, some teachers are allotting time during the day to what are called subject matter centers. Students rotate between areas in the classroom set up for social studies, English, mathematics, and science. At each center, there are specific activities for the children. For example, during a unit on geology, the science center might have examples of rock specimens that the students are expected to examine and identify. Another group might be making maps at the social studies center while a classroom library and comfortable seating might provide the children the opportunity for independent reading during their time in the reading center. For math, there might be problems involving concrete items such as an abacus. College students are introduced to the possibility of creating learning centers during their methods courses. Such an approach to teaching and learning is certainly related to the theory espoused by progressive educators.

Finally, almost every teacher education student is required to take a course in educational psychology. These classes focus on the stages of child development and how these periods in the students' lives affect their learning. Among the theories included in such courses would be constructivism.

It is identified in one textbook as "an educational theory that emphasizes hands-on, activity-based teaching and learning."[8] The primary professional organization for educational psychologists is the American Psychological Association. This group encourages:

> teachers to reconsider the manner in which they view teaching. The APA contends that students are active learners who should be given opportunities to develop their own frames of thought. Teaching techniques should include a variety of different learning activities during which students are free to infer and discover their own answers to important questions. Teachers need to spend time designing these learning situations rather than lecturing. Learning is considered the active framing of personal meaning (by the learner) rather than framing someone else's meaning (which belongs to the teacher).[9]

Needless to say, this point of view, which is frequently a theme in educational psychology classes, is in keeping with the ideas inherent in progressive education.

In almost every education class, students will be introduced to some phase of progressive education theory. At the same time, in college classes outside of the education department, they are most likely to be taught using traditional methods that would be dominated by teacher lectures. Even though this is the case, these lecture classes frequently now include additional visual stimuli such as PowerPoint and, in smaller classes, the opportunity for dialogue between the students and the instructor. Most college teachers outside of the teacher education department have taken few if any education classes, and they might have very little knowledge or even interest in alternative teaching methods. Even though this is the case, many of them are brilliant teachers who are able to hold college students' interest and to inspire them in an academic discipline. Along with teacher education instructors, these professors are also role models for future teachers and their influence can be even more profound than the teacher education instructors. It is also true that some education department faculty continue to use the lecture method even when teaching about such methods as cooperative learning and student projects. John Dewey himself was guilty of only using the lecture method in his college classes. At the same time, unfortunately, some instructors outside of the field of education disparage the education departments in their college and even sometimes attempt to persuade students majoring in their discipline to forget about education courses altogether.

For some colleges and universities, the charge is also made that the teacher education department has been made a "cash cow" for their institution. In the words of John Merrow, these colleges are guilty of "diverting tuition paid by education majors into law, medicine, engineering, and nursing programs." Well-known teacher educator Linda Darling-Hammond has been quoted as saying, "if you are preparing to be a teacher, you can expect half of the tuition money that you put into the till to come back to support your preparation."[10] In such colleges, the teacher education departments may be pressured to utilize more adjuncts or part-time professors and to pay their professors less than in other fields. Merrow goes on to say that "it's no secret that schools of education are at the bottom of the university pecking order. On the bottom rung of the education school's own ladder of prestige are those who actually train teachers."[11]

Considering the salaries of college teachers, a survey taken in 2002 lists the five lowest-paying categories. The very lowest salaries are paid to the teachers of English composition. Next would be instructors in the field of speech, followed by those in health and physical education. Fourth on the list would be general teacher education faculty members.[12]

If teacher education professors and programs lack respect in their institution, one might also ask, do students have negative feelings about the programs? In some cases, education professors are criticized by students for not practicing what they preach. Like John Dewey, they might give lectures about the need to seek student engagement but do not model such techniques in their own classes. For example, an instructor might talk about cooperative learning but never have his or her students working in groups. There is also a frequent charge that there is considerable overlapping in the content of teacher education courses. Still, it is true that in many colleges, future teachers most enjoy and look forward to their education courses.

However, the influence of a student's education classes is often undermined by his or her previous educational experiences. Most teacher education students have been fairly successful academically prior to attending college. They have been able to earn decent grades in classes that were taught most often in a traditional manner. A good many of them have positive memories about their experiences in traditional classes, especially if they have had teachers whom they consider outstanding. It is very likely that they might model their own teaching style on such a person.

It is also true that in their classroom experiences in college, they have been exposed to a number of exceptional traditional teachers. When they student teach, it might well be with a teacher who is not particularly interested in progressive education methods. Especially in today's high school, student teachers will encounter many master teachers whose primary goal is to "cover the material." As pressure increases as a result of the tests mandated by No Child Left Behind, it is possible that future teachers will find even less opportunity to observe progressive education lessons during their student teaching. Thus, a student may have learned a variety of teaching techniques in their education classes but not be in a position to use them during student teaching. Even when they begin teaching in their own classroom, first-year teachers will be affected by the way their fellow teachers are teaching. It is quite possible that they will have a mentor teacher who is conservative in his or her methods. If "teaching to the test" is the primary approach used in a school, a new teacher will find it extremely difficult to experiment with innovative instructional strategies.

All of these mitigating factors can minimize the long-range impact of college teacher education programs. At the same time, it is true that an inspiring teacher education professor can still have a significant influence on his or her students. Such teachers are most often urging their students to treat children as individuals and to use a variety of teaching techniques. Although it is impossible to determine the long-term effect of teacher education programs, as long as progressive education ideas remain in the forefront of teacher education curricula, progressive education will not become obsolete. Along with the impact of these programs, there are several other factors that might help to keep alive progressive ideas in our nation's schools. One such trend in the last fifty years has been the growing popularity of middle schools.

NOTES

1. Kenneth H. Hansen, *Public Education in American Society*, (Englewood Cliffs, NJ: Prentice-Hall, Inc., 1956), 304.

2. Robert Gray Holland, *To Build a Better Teacher*, (Westport, CT: Praeger, 2004), xvii–xviii.

3. Nathan Glazer, "The Trouble with Ed Schools," *Education Next* at http://www.educationnext.org/20053/82.html (accessed 28 September 2005), 2.

4. George R. Cressman and Harold W. Benda, *Public Education in America*, (New York: Appleton-Century-Crofts, 1966), 157–58.

5. Myra Pollack Sadker and David Miller Sadker, *Teachers, Schools, and Society*, (Boston: McGraw Hill, 2005), 315.

6. Allan C. Ornstein and Daniel U. Levine, *Foundations of Education*, (Boston: Houghton Mifflin, 2006), 103.

7. "Motivational Quotes for Teachers," at http://www.pitt.edu/~poole/ARCHIVE#.HTML (accessed 14 March 2005), 2.

8. James A. Johnson, Victor L. Dupuis, Dianne Musial, Gene E. Hall, and Donna M. Gollnick, *Introduction to the Foundations of Education*, (Boston: Allyn and Bacon, 1996), 400.

9. Johnson, Dupuis, Musial, Hall, and Gollnick, *Introduction to the Foundations of Education*, 400.

10. John Merrow, *Choosing Excellence*, (Boston: Scarecrow Press, Inc., 2001), 88.

11. Merrow, *Choosing Excellence*, 85–86.

12. Sharon Walsh, "Law Professors Again Get Top Pay, Faculty-Salary Survey Finds," *The Chronicle of Higher Education*, 12 August 2002, at http://chronicle.com/daily/2002/08/2002081201n.htm (accessed 12 August 2001).

12

Middle Schools

School districts began to establish middle schools in the early 1950s. By the end of the century "the number of schools with a middle-school organization (i.e., grades 5–8 or 6–8)" grew "from 23 percent in 1971 to 69 percent in 2000." Three years ago, a national survey of "K–8 schools found that 84 percent of K–8 respondents," thought that "the ideal grade organization for middle school students is a separately organized middle school."[1] By the end of the twentieth century, there were over twelve thousand middle schools in the United States.[2] It is true that since the passage of No Child Left Behind with its accountability mandates, middle schools and the theories that support them have come under fire. Despite this fact, middle schools continue to remain a popular form of school organization.

The way schools have been organized by grade levels has seen many changes during our history. Until the mid-1830s most schools were privately financed by tuition paid for by parents. Frequently but not always, these schools were organized into a one-room schoolhouse with children of all ages. In most parts of the country, the early schools were established and managed by a Christian religious denomination. Beginning in the mid-1830s, as a result of the leadership of Horace Mann in Massachusetts along with other public school advocates, tax-supported elementary or common schools were established. Later in the century, private academies or high schools began to be converted into public high schools.[3]

In 1909, the Columbus, Ohio Board of Education opened a three-year intermediate school which they called a "junior high." A second such school was established a year later in Berkeley, California. By the 1930s, the junior high school organizational pattern, which included grades 7–9, was found in districts across the United States. This was especially true in midsized and large districts. Some smaller communities still had grades K–12 in one building or have separate schools for students in grades K–6 and 7–12. The newly formed junior high schools were most often patterned after the high schools in their district in that students passed from class to class and had a separate teacher for each subject. The curricula in the junior high were slightly more varied in that there were often mandated classes in shop for boys and home economics for girls. In addition, there were frequently required classes in music and art. Especially in the 7–12 buildings, the younger students attended the same social events, had the same schedule, and rode the same bus as the older high school students. They also shared the same cafeteria, gym, and lavatories. If there were twelfth graders smoking in those lavatories, it was likely that the seventh graders might pick up the same habits. Even in the separate junior high school buildings, the students were often treated as if they were in high school.

As a result, by the midpoint of the twentieth century, a great deal was being written in educational journals about the need to provide a better transition for children as they passed from the security of the self-contained elementary classroom, with one teacher, to the more confusing and impersonal multiple teacher pattern of junior high schools or junior-senior high schools (grades 7–12). The theory underlying the need for the change was based on the developmental differences between elementary and high school students. It was argued that children in grades 5–8 had different psychological and educational needs than either elementary or high school students. In establishing schools for these children, it was thought that a number of steps could be taken to provide a more age-appropriate learning environment. The hope was that schools could be created that would better deal with such problems as "dropouts, teenage pregnancy, and drug and alcohol abuse."[4]

A number of middle schools developed curriculum patterns that were more like those used in the elementary schools. At least in theory many believed that:

the middle-school curriculum should focus on the psychological development of early adolescents and deal with issues related to health, social responsibility, basic communication, and human relations. The development
of more complex thinking skills should be at center stage because, developmentally speaking, many preadolescents are just entering into the Piaget-
ian stage of formal operations, which stresses hypothetical thinking. The academic subject areas of the curriculum should not be disciplinary, but
should aim at socio-personal issues that speak to life interest, peer relations,
questions of social identity, and the like. And exploratory learning should be
valued as a way to open the world up to the preadolescent and to develop
early interest in various new ideas and subjects.[5]

In an article published by the National Association of Elementary
School Principals, it was noted that a middle school should also be concerned about these additional characteristics that are consistent with the
ideas of progressive educators. Effective middle schools should:

- engage every student in a relevant, challenging, integrative, and exploratory curriculum environment that fosters respectful and supportive relationships among students, faculty, families, and the community;
- make learning decisions based on data that go beyond single test results;
- build connections between the community and school that expand
  and enhance the educational opportunities of all students;
- utilize varied teaching and learning approaches;
- provide a flexible organizational structure;
- provide programs that foster health, wellness, and safety[6]

Another trend that in part relates to the objectives of progressive educators is the growing practice of dividing schools with large student pop-
ulations into "schools within a school." The purpose of such an approach
is to create a more "child-centered" environment and to develop a more
comfortable "learning community" for children. In these more intimate
school settings, teachers are frequently involved in interdisciplinary curricula and team-teaching. Unlike many junior high schools, students in
these schools are usually heterogeneously grouped rather than the more
traditional method of ability grouping. Teachers are given time during the

school day for planning. Guidance and counseling opportunities are an important service offered by the school. According to middle-school theory, parental involvement is also strongly encouraged.[7]

In carrying out these goals that are inherent in the middle-school concept, these programs should:

> emphasize problem-solving skills, reflective thinking processes, and individualized learning programs. Curriculum content is easily integrated, and the emphasis on instruction is that the teacher is a personal guide and facilitator of learning as opposed to a dispenser of knowledge. . . . There is a decreased emphasis on content and competition so commonly found in the junior and senior high school.[8]

Indeed there are schools that do appear to follow closely the progressive theories of middle-school advocates. One such school that has been highlighted in a popular textbook is the Shoreham-Wading Middle School that is located on Long Island in New York State. The book quotes a thirteen-year-old student who describes his school as follows. "It blew me away when I moved here in time for 6th grade. . . . In my old school it was like being in prison, but this school is comfortable. It's like being at home. The teachers get to know you well, and there's enough happening to keep you busy all the time. I really like it here."[9] Gene I. Maeroff, a former *New York Times* reporter who is now a senior fellow at the Carnegie Foundation for the Advancement of Teaching, observed the following while visiting the school:

- Team teaching
- Extensive use of experimental learning
- Cooperative or group learning
- Frequent teacher team planning
- Teachers eating lunch with their students every day
- Community service acting as part of the curriculum
- Students working on a small farm owned by the school
- Frequent field trips exploring career options
- Mixed grouping in almost all classes
- Some students training in conflict management to help their peers resolve their disputes

- School psychologist encountering only three cases of hardcore drug use among students during his fifteen years of working at the school
- School exemplifying John Dewey's contention that a sense of community—what Dewey called "the moving spirit of the whole group"—can lead to order when everyone has a chance to feel a part of the enterprise[10]

This progressive school model is certainly not found in every middle school. In a speech before a group of middle-school educators, M. Hayes Mizell pointed out that the National Forum to Accelerate Middle Grade Reform was finding it "difficult to identify middle schools that met the qualitative criteria we should expect of every school with grades 6, 7 and 8." What the group was looking for were schools that clearly demonstrate "academic excellence," which are "developmentally responsive" and "socially equitable."[11] It is the view of Mizzel and other critics that middle schools generally are not living up to their potential. In explaining this conclusion, the following factors were identified.

- Many school boards, school administrators, and teachers do not really understand middle-school theory. As a result, their schools, which might be called middle schools, differ little from a traditional junior high.
- Some middle schools have gone so far in attempting to meet students' developmental needs that they have sacrificed academics. "It is not learning, but sympathy for students that sets these schools' agenda." As a result, curricula and academic standards have declined in some middle schools.[12]
- Too many middle-school teachers are not prepared academically to teach in the areas they have been assigned.[13]

On a more hopeful note, it should be understood that although these criticisms do have some validity, changes are taking place in middle-school education. Many states are now requiring separate certification for middle-school teachers. To obtain certification as a middle-school teacher, future teachers are required to take classes in such areas as child and adolescent development, middle-school teaching methods, or middle-school theory. The National Middle School Association has been created, and it currently publishes an influential journal to help disseminate information and ideas related to middle-school education. As a result of this and other organizations, along with numerous books on the subject, a philosophical justification for middle schools has been created.

By 1990, there was an emerging consensus among professional educators in the United States that children of middle-school age have special educational needs. The Carnegie Corporation published in 1989 a report titled *Turning Points: Preparing American Youth for the 21st Century.* Among the observations contained in this document was this statement:

> There is a crucial need to help adolescents at this early age to acquire durable self-esteem, flexible and inquiring habits of mind, reliable and relatively close human relationships, a sense of belonging in a valued group, and a sense of usefulness in some way beyond the self. They need to find constructive expression of their inherent curiosity and exploratory energy; and they need a basis for making informed, deliberate decisions-especially on matters that have large consequences, such as educational futures and drug use.[14]

To support these goals it has been suggested that middle schools adopt the following practices:

- incorporating the questions and concerns of students into the curriculum;
- interdisciplinary team organization;
- extended range of teaching strategies, including use of cooperative learning activities;
- flexible scheduling, including block schedules; and
- exploratory activities and courses[15]

As we enter the twenty-first century, it appears that there a consensus on the appropriate goals and methods necessary for an effective middle-school education. This agreement is very much in keeping with many of the tenets of progressive education. The reality of the middle-school movement does not necessarily reflect the hoped-for changes inherent in the middle-school theory. One report issued in the 1990s concluded that "the vast majority of schools housing early adolescents especially in cities, resemble the junior highs they were supposed to reform."[16]

Progress toward the goals of the middle-school movement also have recently faced a major new obstacle. With the advent of "high-stakes testing," especially as it is now required in grades 3–8 by the No Child Left Behind Act, the academic achievement levels of middle-school students have come under serious scrutiny. As the mandated tests under the law were instituted during the 2005–2006 school year, it can be assured that concerns about scores will undoubtedly heighten.

The Alliance for Excellent Education in June of 2005 included the following warnings concerning high-stakes testing. Twenty-eight percent of those students entering ninth grade in September 2005 are in danger of becoming dropouts in large part because they do not have the necessary reading skills. The study also claims that only 34 percent of those entering ninth grade will graduate from high school in four years with the knowledge that they need for success in college.[17]

President Bush has taken note of such statistics and included in his 2005 State of the Union Address his opinion that the testing requirements of No Child Left Behind should be expanded at the secondary-school level. If such a proposal were enacted, it is quite possible that there would be more pressure on middle schools to give additional emphasis to preparing students for tests.[18] Although Congress presently has shown little support for adding to the required tests, the issue is far from dead.

The results of the standards movement, high-stakes testing, and increased school accountability are apparently already affecting middle schools. It has been reported that because tests are currently only required in language arts and mathematics, that other subjects are being given less instructional time. These two tests and the consequences of the scores and the importance ascribed to the students' scores would also seem to be forcing "administrators, especially in those schools where students have not tested well, into making drastic changes in curriculum." It has been claimed that many of the curricular changes that have been made to accommodate the new tests have not been carefully considered, and, as a result, the quality of the curriculum has not been improved.[19]

Forcing curriculum changes based on the new tests has resulted in some outcomes that are contrary to the accepted goals of middle schools. Among the concerns of middle-school supporters are the following:

- Using a single indicator (a written test) to judge a student's learning is unfair. Alternative methods of assessment should be used.
- The pressure on schools is forcing them to use valuable instructional time on teaching test-taking skills.

- The content of the curriculum is being narrowed to what is likely to be tested.[20]

At the same time, the provisions of the No Child Left Behind Act potentially could improve academic instruction at the middle-school level. The requirement that schools have "highly qualified teachers," if it can be enforced, should help middle schools. It is in these schools where we have the highest percentage of teachers who are uncertified in the academic area they are teaching. It has been claimed that in high-poverty middle schools that "more than 50 percent of the classes are taught by teachers who did not major in the course subject."[21]

Whether a new group of teachers who are better prepared in their academic areas can and will also accept the educational philosophy of the middle-school movement remains an open question. There are those who worry that our emphasis on tests will force teachers to only teach "things that can be measured 'objectively,' preferably with an easy-to-grade standardized test." These critics believe that this type of test "holds teachers and students accountable for mastering only skills and knowledge that are established and uncontroversial" and that require only "a single correct answer. As a result, students are not encouraged or allowed to explore the ambiguous, the uncertain, the mysterious—the wonders of the world." Critics of standardized tests believe that our reliance on testing is "killing off the qualities our children need most to appeal to future employers." These characteristics include "innovation, initiative, and flexibility."[22] It has also been pointed out that the once-admired Japanese educational system is in the process of reforming their schools that have "long relied on a uniform national curriculum and after-hours classes at Juku 'cram schools.'" The Japanese now appear to believe that "this approach has stifled creativity, innovation, independent thinking, contributing to the stagnation of the Japanese economy."[23]

Others point to the difficult position of middle-school leaders in our society. They are being pushed to focus on test scores even when they personally believe that other elements of school life are equally important. School-board surveys have also shown that the morale of teachers and school administrators is low.[24] The challenge for the middle-school movement in the United States is to somehow maintain its primary objective of providing an age-appropriate school environment to help students in their passage from elementary school to high school. Such an environment undoubtedly includes many of the goals and objectives called for by progressive educators. Still, it is essential that even if schools are able to use the techniques inherent in progressive education, these schools must do a better job in teaching basic learning skills. To do both will be a formidable task, but schools are trying.

After reading the *Turning Points: Preparing American Youth for the 21st Century* report referred to earlier, one school in an urban community in Michigan is indeed trying to use creative progressive education methods to teach the basic skills. A group of parents, administrators, and community members has developed "a standards based curriculum which will be taught using a progressive education model." The thematic units that have been created integrate the arts into a curriculum that has been well-received by both students and teachers. At the outset of their effort to write such a curriculum, the group agreed on the following goals for their middle school. They would:

- Transfer current middle-level educational research and theory into practice
- Involve community partnerships
- Employ integrated thematic units
- Create teams for program planning and implementation
- Choose from a variety of appropriate teaching models[25]

In carrying out these goals the school is seeking to use the arts to allow the students to "explore human creativity." For this school, the initial results have been encouraging to all of the stakeholders. Test scores have improved by 15 percent in reading and 18 percent in math, and the school has developed a waiting list of parents wishing to enroll their children.[26]

Other states and individual school districts are also seeking ways to maintain the progressive elements of middle-school theory while at the same time raising test scores. In New York State, some middle schools are being given flexibility in meeting the state curriculum requirements in order to allow these schools to find unique ways to accomplish this goal as well as to improve test scores. Other districts have actually given up on the middle-school model because of the poor test scores. Several major cities have reorganized their schools into either a K–8 design or a 7–12 organization. Still, it would seem that there remains "among adults who

work with young adolescents" a "broad, widely shared philosophy about
the needs of these youth and how best to meet these needs." As a result,
there is now a major effort in our nation to make the necessary changes in
our current middle schools so that they can successfully meet the challenge of the No Child Left Behind legislation. Examples of some of the
work that is being done can be found in *An Educator's Guide to School-
wide Reform*, published by the Educational Research Service. The same
agency has also created three other guides:

1. *Blueprints for School Success: A Guide to New American School
   Designs*
2. *Comprehensive Models for School Improvement: Finding the Right
   Match and Making it Work*
3. *Handbook on Improving Student Achievement*[27]

Despite the efforts taking place to accommodate middle-school theory to
the challenges created by the No Child Left Behind law, there will be increasing pressures on schools to use traditional teaching approaches at the
middle-school level. As in other grades, there will be a perceived need by
teachers to "cover" content and to "teach to the test." At the same time, we
now have almost fifty years of history with middle-school theory that has
supported progressive education methods. The question remains whether
or not we, as a society, can prepare students for challenging academic tests
and also incorporate classroom experiences that will enhance students' creativity and help them to become problem solvers. The answer to this question will have impact on the future of progressive education and whether
or not it will be a major factor in how we teach our young people in the
twenty-first century. Another issue that will undoubtedly have an impact on
the future of progressive education is the concept of school choice. The effects of our national fascination with this idea will also help determine the
nature of our educational programs in the years ahead.

NOTES

1. "Research in Support of Middle Level Grade Configuration" at http://
www.nmsa.org/portals/0/pdf/research/Research_Briefs/grade_configuration.pdf
(accessed 20 January 2006), 1.

2. James A. Johnson, Victor L. Dupuis, Dianne Musial, Gene E. Hall, and Donna M. Gollnick, *Introduction to the Foundations of Education*, (Boston: Allyn and Bacon, 1996), 444.

3. Myra Pollack Sadker and David Miller Sadker, *Teachers, Schools, and Society*, (Boston: McGraw Hill, 2005), 297.

4. Robert F. McNergney and Joanne M. Herbert, *Foundations of Education*, (Boston: Allyn and Bacon, 1995), 182.

5. Peter S. Hlebowitsh, *Foundations of American Education*, (Belmont, CA: Wadsworth/Thomson Learning, 2001), 340–41.

6. Sue Swain, "What Middle Schools Should and Can Be, at http://naesp .org/ContentLoad.do?contentId=537&action=print (accessed 20 January 2006), 1.

7. "What is a Middle School?" *Arlington Heights School District 25* at http:// www.ahsd25.k12.il.us/Curriculum%20Info/middle.html (accessed 16 November 200), 1–3.

8. Johnson, Dupuis, Musial, Hall, and Gollnick, *Introduction to the Foundations of Education*, 444.

9. McNergney and Herbert, *Foundations of Education*, 183.

10. McNergney and Herbert, *Foundations of Education*, 183.

11. M. Hayes Mizzel, "Thirty and Counting" at http://www.middleweb.com/ HMsouth.html (accessed 16 November 2005), 1–2.

12. Mizzel, "Thirty and Counting," 2.

13. Mizzel, "Thirty and Counting," 5.

14. *"Turning Points" Preparing American Youth for the 21st Century*, Report of the Task Force on Education of Young Adolescents, Carnegie Council on Adolescent Development (New York: Carnegie Corporation of New York, 1989), 12.

15. Kevin and James M. Cooper, *Those Who Can, Teach*, (Boston: Houghton Mifflin Company, 1995), 169.

16. Larry Cuban, "What Happens to Reforms That Last? The Case of the Junior High School," *The American Educational Research Journal*, 29, no. 2 (Summer 1992): 246.

17. "28% of America's 8th Graders at Risk of Not Graduating High School, According to Alliance for Excellent Education," *Alliance for Excellent Education*, at http://www.all4ed.org/press/pr_060205.html (accessed 14 January 2006), 1.

18. "President Recognizes Needs of Middle and High School Students in State of the Union Address," *Alliance for Excellent Education*, at http://www.all4ed .org/press/pr_012104.html (accessed 14 January 2006), 1.

19. Kenneth E. Vogler, "An Integrated Curriculum Using State Standards in a High-Stakes Testing Environment," *Middle School Journal*, at http://www.nmsa .org/Publications/MiddleSchoolJournal/March2003/Article1/tabid/145/Default.a spx (accessed 14 January 2006), 1.

20. Vogler, "An Integrated Curriculum Using State Standards in a High-Stakes Testing Environment," 2.

21. "Alliance for Excellent Education Releases Report on NCLB & Middle Schools," *Alliance for Excellent Education*, at http://www.educationnews.org/alliance_for_excellent_education.htm (accessed 20 January 2006), 1.

22. Barbara Klein, John D. McNeil, and Lynn A. Stout, "The Achievement Trap," *Education Week*, at http://www.edweek.org/ew/articles/2005/11/16/12klein.h25.html (accessed 18 November 2005), 1.

23. Klein, McNeil, and Stout, "The Achievement Trap," 2.

24. Jean Johnson, "It's Time to Address the Human Factor in Education Reform," *Public Agenda*, at http://publicagenda.org/aboutpa/aboutpa_articles_detail.cfm?list=25 (accessed 18 November 2005), 1.

25. Karen Bolak, Donna Bialach, and Maureen Dunphy, "Standards-Based, Thematic Units Integrate the Arts and Energize Students and Teachers," *Middle School Journal*, at http://www.nmsa.org/Publications/MiddleSchoolJournal/May2005/Article2/tabid/122/Default.aspx (accessed 14 January 2006), 3.

26. Bolak, Bialach, and Dunphy, "Standards-Based, Thematic Units Integrate the Arts and Energize Students and Teachers," 7.

27. M. Hayes Mizzel, "Middle School Reform: Where Are We Now?" at http://www.middleweb.com/HMFndMidS.html (accessed 16 November 2005), 4.

13

Choice

The purpose of this chapter will be to focus on the current and future impact of choice programs on progressive education. Advocates of giving parents the opportunity to select their child's school have argued that it will encourage innovative school programs. Even if most public schools continue to concentrate on traditional curriculum and teaching methods, choice would prevent a monopoly of these traditional approaches and allow at least some parents to select a progressive school setting. Thus, theoretically, school choice could stimulate the growth of progressive education in the United States.

It is true that there has always been some form of school choice in this country. Even after the growth of the public-school movement in the nineteenth century, there have always been private schools available. These options have included both religious and secular schools. Of course, because these institutions relied on tuition, many families were unable to truly have a choice. As a result, the free public schools enrolled at least 90 percent of our nation's students by the beginning of the twenty-first century.

In 1955, economist Milton Friedman introduced the idea of government-funded vouchers to be used by parents to pay for their child's education at a public or private school. He argued that "such schools would be conducted under a variety of auspices: by private enterprises operated for profit, nonprofit institutions established by private endowment, religious bodies, and some even by governmental units."[1] Friedman, a well-known economist, believes that vouchers would create a healthy competition in the field of education. He has argued that because private school options are available only to those who can afford the tuition, the public schools have had a virtual monopoly on most school-age students. Without equal competition, the public schools have had little motivation to improve their product. Just as the competition in our capitalist economy creates increased efficiency and higher quality goods and services, the same would be true in the field of education.

This idea was introduced two years before the Russian launching of Sputnik created a period when Americans would begin to look more closely at the perceived weaknesses of the public schools. Still there was little or no movement toward any form of choice during the 1950s. When the idea reemerged in the 1960s, it was not the rather radical approach of a voucher plan, but a more modest reform known as magnet schools. Although magnet schools created some competition within a school district, a primary motivation for many boards of education was to find a way to bring about additional racial integration. This was especially true in a number of urban areas where the neighborhood concept of school attendance was already creating segregated school systems. Magnet schools have been defined as "schools offering specialized and unique programs designed to attract students from throughout the district." By the turn of the century there were 1,372 magnet schools located in thirty-three states.[2]

These magnet schools frequently focused on such areas as the arts, science, or vocational education. Other districts established honors high schools for outstanding students, and some developed schools that stressed progressive education ideas. Created primarily at the high-school level, there are also choices for magnet schools at the elementary and middle school level.

It is important to note that magnet schools remained totally under the control of the district's board of education and administration. These institutions are required to teach the curriculum prescribed by their state and to follow all state and local guidelines. This includes giving the same standardized tests as other schools in the district. The only difference is that magnet schools placed a conscious emphasis on a particular subject or educational approach. A school for the arts offers a large variety of electives in music and art. The music program has multiple performance groups. While other city high schools might not have a string program or a school orchestra, a school for the arts would present such an opportunity. A school such as this, unlike many magnet options, is likely to have entrance requirements such as an audition for music students or the submission of a portfolio for an art applicant. Where the district established an honors high school, students had to have achieved a certain grade point average and perhaps receive recommendations from former teachers. Other choices, such as vocational education magnets, have few if any requirements.

It was hoped that the magnet option would cause African-American students, who might otherwise attend a neighborhood comprehensive high school that was highly segregated, to choose to travel across the city to a more integrated school for the arts. Although it is difficult to determine, it seems that, at least initially, magnet schools created some additional integration. As the number of Caucasians continues to decline, truly integrated schools that represent the racial breakdown in the nation have become impossible. There are just not enough white children to go around in most of our cities.

At the same time, these schools do offer students a real choice. For the purpose of this chapter, the question becomes, do magnet schools in any way foster the continuation and growth of progressive education theory and methods? In attempting to answer this question, one must begin with the realization that these schools are required to teach the same curriculum as any other public school. Their students must take the same high-stakes tests, and the schools will be held accountable to the public for the results of these tests. It is also true that most magnet schools do focus on an academic area rather than any overriding educational theory such as progressive education. A magnet high school of science is, in most cases, probably a school that is dominated by traditional teacher-centered instructional methods.

There are though, magnet schools that do focus on a specific educational theory. An example would be those districts that allow Montessori classes as an option. In the Rochester, New York, community there are several magnet schools whose programs are very much in the progressive tradition. One such school is the Quest Elementary School. One of the three elementary schools in the Hilton Central School District, a small suburban district of Rochester, New York, the Quest school has been since 1994 a school of choice which appears to be prospering. Although the district ensures that this school has the same percentage of special education students as the other two elementary schools, test scores of the Quest students are the highest in the district. Of course, because the new required tests in grades 3–8 are being offered for the first time in 2006, it remains to be seen whether the school can maintain its lead in test scores at every grade level. The results of these tests will be especially interesting because teachers at the school are adamant in claiming that they are not "teaching to any test." Observing the school in operation, one cannot deny that it has a different approach to teaching and learning than one would find in a traditional elementary school.

What makes the Quest school unique is the organization of its students. They are not placed in traditional grade-level classes but rather in an ungraded setting that finds students who might ordinarily be in grades 1–3 working together as one group. The same is true of children who might be in separate classes for grades 4–6. A publication of the school district explains how the school is organized into a multiage environment in which a group of children of various ages work together. They are "individually growing at a pace that is developmentally appropriate, in one learning community." In the same pamphlet, the principal of the school is quoted as saying that "students enjoy their discoveries, take ownership of their learning, and have pride in their success." Other goals of the school include having students collaborate with others and learn to use "various strategies" to understand themselves as learners. It is noted that Quest teachers will "establish a democratic environment where all voices will be heard while fostering mutual respect." Progressive educators in any generation would applaud the mission statement of the Hilton Central School District, which states in part that it is the goal of the district's schools to help students to become "self-directed, life-long learners who think critically and creatively and function as caring, responsible, productive citizens."[3]

In the Hilton school district's *Community Handbook*, the authors have chosen to quote Jean Piaget, who has written that:

> In order for a child to understand something, he must construct it himself. . . . Every time we teach a child something, we keep him from re-inventing it for himself. . . . That which we allow him to discover by himself will remain with him visible . . . for the rest of his life.[4]

That this is a magnet school seeking to function in the progressive tradition is clear, and it is only one of such schools in the Rochester area. Another is a secondary school located in the city of Rochester called the School Without Walls. The school's website offers the following description of their high school. It is claimed that the school:

- Practices a learner-centered interdisciplinary philosophy in which the needs and interest of students, as well as the demands of society, form the curriculum.
- Emphasizes critical thinking and responsible citizenship and honors all students' learning styles.
- Expects students to become responsible for their own learning.
- Requires students to give back to the community through two and a half hours of volunteer service each week.
- Provides opportunities for all students to be involved in the management of the school and in the decision-making and problem solving of important school issues.[5]

In carrying out this philosophy, the school has been able to send 85 percent of its graduates to college. This is considerably higher than other high schools in the city. At the same time, it has maintained one of the district's highest attendance rates and lowest suspension rates. Perhaps most impressive is that it has had one of the highest success rates with "at-risk-of-failure" students.[6] While the schools described above do not represent the majority of magnet schools, the fact that these schools are using progressive theory and methods might lead one to conclude that choice is helping to keep alive the progressive education tradition.

Currently an even more popular form of choice that has evolved more recently are the so-called charter schools. This form of school organization is similar to the older magnet-school concept, but there are significant differences. One well-known education textbook "defines a charter school as being an independent public school supported by state funds, but freed from many regulations and run by individuals who have the power to hire and to fire colleagues and to budget money as they see fit.[7] Originally suggested by Albert Shanker, the former president of the American Federation of Teachers, charter schools, unlike magnets, are free from most of the state and local regulations. They are free to design their own program and to implement it as they see fit.

Once a state has authorized the formation of charter schools, the application procedure is introduced. An individual or a group can then submit an application to create their own charter school. In the application, those seeking a charter must articulate in detail their educational plan and an acceptable process for assessing student learning. In addition, applicants must have appropriate housing for their school. Because charter schools are still publicly financed, they cannot have a religious orientation. In most states, it is also required that the school plan for significant parental involvement. The schools are free in most cases to hire a number of uncertified teachers, and they also can devise a calendar and school day that are different from the other public schools in their district. It is not unusual for charter schools to have additional instructional time. Like magnet schools, a charter might well give to its school a special focus. Some might advertise a "back-to-basics approach" while others could attempt to create a school in the progressive tradition.

When a charter is granted by the state, it is for a specific period of time, such as five years. During the final year of the charter, the school must demonstrate that their students have achieved acceptable academic progress. The state and perhaps the local district will then make a decision whether to recharter the school for an additional period. Families who wish their children to attend a charter school in their district must first register their child. If the school has more applicants than they can accept, some form of lottery system is conducted. Charter schools are not in most cases allowed to have specific entrance requirements. Although charters have evolved in different ways in various states, increasingly it is private, for-profit companies who seek charters. Often this is done at the request of individuals in a community who are seeking alternative educational choices for the children of the district.

Most of the 3,600 charter schools that have been established are now found in larger urban or suburban districts. Nationally, teacher unions as well as groups representing school administrators and boards of education have been less than enthusiastic about the expansion of charter schools. It would seem that these groups are primarily concerned that these new district schools will drain students and funds from the traditional schools in the district. Most state laws grant charter schools the same per-pupil aid as the other public schools in the district at the same grade levels. Thus, if a district is spending nine thousand dollars per student at the elementary level, a new elementary charter school would receive that amount for each of its students. Unlike other district schools, a committee of parents, administrators, and teachers determines how money is spent on each budget category. Because charter-school teachers are not part of a union or a state retirement system, these schools' committees have much more latitude in determining salaries, fringe benefits, and other expenditures. When the school is managed by a for-profit company, many of these decisions are made by corporate officials.

As early as 1995, ten pilot charter schools were agreed upon in the city of Boston. Unlike later charter schools, these pilots had the support of the Boston teachers' union. "Most of the ten were progressive in the Deweyan sense." These schools are still functioning in the city, but the number of progressive options has not grown during the last ten years.[8] Another interesting experiment is now taking place in New York City. The teachers' union itself has gained a charter to operate a school. Some observers have commented that "the success or failure of this charter school could affect attempts to unionize charter schools at a time when teachers' unions have been ambivalent at best about such schools."[9]

While states continue to authorize additional charter schools, it is difficult to predict whether this trend will encourage or discourage the development of schools employing progressive theories and methods. Because the schools often have a relatively short period of time to prove themselves, there is significant pressure on them to demonstrate academic improvement. Since the measurement of success is usually based in large part on test scores, it would seem that most charter schools would be tempted to adopt more traditional instructional models that are associated with the transfer of knowledge. If the tests used to gauge how well charter schools are doing emphasize the knowledge of facts rather than the students' abilities to solve problems in a creative way, it is hard to conceive of programs that do not emphasize preparation for the test. Still it is quite possible that there are enough parents and educators who are committed to innovation that there will continue to be charter schools that are truly different.

Another form of organization that offers parents a choice is open enrollment. When a larger district is willing to forgo the traditional method of assigning students to a neighborhood school, they can make it possible to give parents an option to seek attendance in a public school located in another section of the school district. Not without logistic problems, such a plan allows an opportunity to offer a progressive school or schools for those families who are willing to have their children travel outside their neighborhood to attend school. Again this type of system can encourage those who advocate something other than a traditional program to have a choice.

Overall it would seem that magnet schools, charter schools, and open enrollment would not hinder the survival of progressive education in our public schools. It might even be argued that these types of school choice will have a positive impact in establishing progressive alternatives. In a book titled *Charter Schools*, the authors argue that modern progressive educators "in the tradition of Dewey and Dubois" support choice. They cite Deborah Meier, who believes that "charter schools offer an opportunity to break down factory schools and the factory style of education." She was critical of other progressive educators who opposed charters when she wrote that:

> Progressive policymakers and legislators have on the whole allowed their concern with equity to lead them to reflexively attack choice as inherently elitist. . . . This is, I believe, a grave mistake. The argument over choice, unlike the one over private-school vouchers, offers progressives an opportunity. After all, it wasn't so long ago that progressive educators were enthusiastically supporting schools of choice, usually called alternative schools. These alternatives were always on the fringe, as though the vast majority of schools were doing just fine. We now have a chance to make such alternatives the mainstream—not just for avant-garde "misfits" or "nerds" or "those more at risk."[10]

A number of other progressive educators would agree with Pulitzer Prize–winner Jonathan Kozol, who has argued that "charter schools only isolate the privileged elite." For the critics,

> the charter-school idea, and school choice itself, represents a contemporary, postmodern rejection of the possibility of a common school for all citizens. As a result, they argue, the idea threatens to turn the relationship between society and its educational needs into little more than a commercial transaction based on individual self-interest and competitive self-advantage.[11]

The debate regarding the impact of progressive education on school choice will continue. Supporters of choice have been consistent in arguing that experimentation will be encouraged and that many of the effective practices that are created will be transferred to the traditional public schools. The successful schools of choice could be considered as laboratories that would, among other things, allow for schools embracing a truly progressive theory. In his book *The Charter School Challenge*, Bryan C. Hassel has challenged this "laboratory thesis." After studying the issue, he has concluded that "charter schools are unlikely to transform public education by serving as laboratories for 'good ideas' at the school level."[12] He believes that, "most school districts have already been exposed to the ideas their charter schools are implementing and are choosing not to adopt them."[13]

If progressive educators today differ on the impact of magnet schools and charter schools, they are more united in their opposition to the school voucher plan. There are a number of ways to implement school vouchers. The most common would be the following:

1. *Universal vouchers* allows all parents to direct funds set aside for education by the government to their children to a school of choice, whether the school is public, private, or religious. In effect, separating the government financing of education from the government operation of schools.
2. *Means-tested vouchers* enables income-eligible families, usually in limited numbers, to direct funds set aside for education by the government to pay for tuition at the public, private, or religious school of their choice.
   Examples: Cleveland, Milwaukee
3. *Failing schools vouchers* allows all parents whose children attend public schools identified as failing to direct funds set aside for education by the government to a better-performing public, private, or religious school of their choice. There are no income requirements, and eligibility is based solely on the success of individual public schools.
   Example: Florida[14]

The fiercest debates occur when a proposal is made for a universal voucher format. Rather than introduce all of the arguments for and against such a plan, for our purposes, we will be content to consider the possible impact of such a plan on progressive education in the United States. Should a city, state, or even the nation begin a universal voucher plan, it would seem that the big winners would be private schools. Because vouchers could be used at for-profit schools, elite secular private schools, and those schools sponsored by religious groups, it is true that parents who might not be able or willing to pay tuition for these schools could now consider them for their children. Currently the largest number of private schools in the United States are sponsored by religious denominations. Within this group the biggest percentage is Roman Catholic schools. In recent years there has been an increased number of so-called "Christian schools" that have been established by conservative or fundamentalist denominations. Whether they are Roman Catholic or Protestant, religious schools are not known for their progressive approaches to education. Discipline and order are often emphasized and traditional teaching methods are commonplace. One can go too far with such stereotypes, but there is little evidence that schools sponsored by religious groups are known for their progressive approaches. The same can be said about many of the more elite prep schools. Although some of the schools of choice under a voucher system such as those in the Montessori tradition would be considered progressive, it is hard to see how a voucher system would greatly benefit the theory and practice of progressive education.

As we look to the future, it is difficult to predict whether the nation will embrace the idea of school vouchers. In recent years there have been public referenda and court decisions that have not always been supportive. However, there seems to be growing interest among minorities in cities for the opportunity of using vouchers to pay for a child's education. The Republican Party has been consistent in their support of the idea of school vouchers. Democrats, while accepting charter schools, have not been in favor of such plans. Certainly a factor in the Democratic Party's opposition has been the pressure from their allies in the teachers' unions and other school-related lobbying groups. At this point in our history, one would find it difficult to find justification for predicting a national voucher system.

There is an additional form of choice that continues to grow in the United States. The number of families that are now educating their children at home continues to grow. It is difficult to arrive at an exact number of such children, but the National Home Education Research Institute now estimates that it is close to two million. During the past four years, home-schooling has grown by 30 percent, and it is estimated that it will continue to grow at 15 percent each year. This same group has also predicted that the diversity of homeschool parents will also grow.[15]

To determine the impact of homeschooling on progressive education, it is helpful to know something about the families who are making the choice to educate their children at home. In 1999, one survey showed the following:

- Fifty percent of the children who are homeschooled would have been in grades K–6, 22 percent in middle school (6–8), and 28 percent in high school (9–12).
- Sixty-four percent would come from families with incomes under $50,000 per year.
- Seventy-five percent were white.
- Fifty-two percent were from two-parent homes where only one parent worked.[16]

There are a number of reasons that parents are making the choice to homeschool their children. A survey conducted by the Home School Legal Defense Fund reported the following analysis:

- Religious convictions: 49 percent
- Positive social environment: 15 percent
- Academic excellence: 14 percent
- Specific needs of the child: 12 percent
- Curriculum choice: 5 percent
- Flexibility: 5 percent[17]

Another researcher divided the families choosing homeschooling into two basic categories. One group, called ideologues, "are very focused on imparting their values and view the home as their school, a place where they choose the curricula, create the rules, and enforce the schedules." Member of the other group, which the researcher Van Galen calls the pedagogues, "are motivated by more humanistic educational goals; they are interested in the process as much as the end product of learning. As a group, they are considered more open to various educational strategies.

Pedagogues emphasize intrinsic motivation and experimental activities."[18] The motivation of these two groups is very different, but they are united in their common dissatisfaction with the public schools.

There is undoubtedly a minority of homeschool parents who would be open and supportive of some aspects of progressive education. Those labeled by Van Galen as ideologues are obviously interested in broadening the educational opportunities of their children. One parent writing on the Internet refers to Dewey's influence on his thinking about education. For him at least:

> what struck him most strongly in the context of home schooling is his [Dewey's] emphasis on the child's experience and his call to understand the roles of subject matter and organization within rather than apart from that experience. If we watch our children, we see how their experience of the world is both rich in content and progressively structured from within.[19]

While some parents may have absorbed some progressive theories, most of them have not been trained as teachers. Thus, it is likely that, unlike teacher education students, they have not been exposed to the theories of Dewey and other progressive educators. Like many of the graduates of teacher education programs, they are most likely to revert to the teaching methods of their own former teachers. This could easily include giving their children frequent "worksheets" and other "busywork." More recently, these traditional teaching methods are being altered somewhat as more parents are using computer-based instruction as a major tool.

Whatever the methods used by homeschool parents, there remains a tremendous advantage in that it is most often "one-on-one instruction." It also makes it easier for homeschool teachers to allow their students to proceed at their own pace. These advantages perhaps help to explain the fact that "homeschooled children generally score quite well on standardized tests, averaging between the sixty-fifth and ninetieth percentiles."[20]

Some progressive educators who worry about homeschooling are most concerned with the possibility that these children are being narrowly educated or even worse, indoctrinated in their parents' worldview. The primary concern is with the large number of parents who have been religiously motivated. Others are concerned with the fact that homeschool children are too often lacking opportunities to interact with a diverse group of children. Their social contacts are sometimes primarily with other members of their religious denomination or with other homeschoolers. This type of separation is not consistent with the democratic ideals of most progressive educators.

Homeschooling, despite its growth as an educational choice, will not likely be a dominant force in determining the fate of progressive education. Still, one can conclude that it will continue to be an option for that segment of our population that is seeking a way to provide their children with an alternative to the traditional public schools.

All of the choice options discussed in this chapter can in their own way impact the future of progressive education in the United States. To differing degrees, each affords a way that progressive ideas can be kept alive. Even if this is the case, the dominant educational trends of our day remain the back-to-basics movement, curriculum standards, high-stakes testing, and school accountability. Unless these initiatives can be supplemented by an equally strong commitment to the objectives of progressive educators, we may have indeed seen during the last century the rise and fall of progressive education. Prior to reaching a decision on this question, there are several other factors that might affect the outcome. One such possibility is an area that has been associated with stimulating student creativity and problem solving. That is the area known as gifted and talented education.

NOTES

1. Robert F. McNergney and Joanne M. Herbert, *Foundations of Education*, (Boston: Allyn and Bacon, 1995), 249.

2. Education Commission of the States, "Magnet Schools: Quick Facts," 2004, www.ecs.org/html/IssueSection.asp?issueid=80&s=Quick+Facts (accessed 7 March 2004), 1.

3. "QUEST Elementary School," at www.hilton.k12.ny.us (accessed 30 January 2006), 1.

4. "Hilton Central School Community Handbook" 2005–2006, 4.

5. Rochester City School District, "School Without Walls," http://www.rcsdk 12.org/schools/secondary/sww.htm (accessed 23 January 2006), 1.

6. "School Without Walls," http://www.rcsdk12.org/schools/secondary/sww .htm 1–2.

7. McNergney and Herbert, *Foundations of Education*, 547.

8. Ronald S. Brandt, editor, *Education in a New Era*, (Alexandria,VA: Association for Supervision and Curriculum Development, 2000), 219.

9. "Union-Run Charter School Draws Scrutiny," *CNN.com*, http://www.cnn.com/2006/EDUCATION/01/26/union.charter.school.ap/index.html (accessed 26 January 2006), 1.

10. Danny Weil, *Charter Schools*, (Santa Barbara, CA: ABC-CLIO Inc., 2000), 123.

11. Weil, *Charter Schools*, 122.

12. Bryan C. Hassel, *The Charter School Challenge*, (Washington, DC: Brookings Institution Press, 1999), 133.

13. Hassel, *The Charter School Challenge*, 131.

14. "Vouchers," *Milton & Rose D. Friedman Foundation*, at www.friedman-foundation.org/schoolchoice/index.html (accessed 7 March 2004), 1.

15. Barbara Martin, "Home Education: The Movement and Methods," at http://www.thehomeschoolmagazine.com/how-to-homeschool/articles/articles.php?aid=197 (accessed 27 January 2006), 2.

16. Myra Pollack Sadker and David Miller Sadker, *Teachers, Schools, and Society*, (Boston: McGraw Hill, 2005), 157.

17. Joel Spring, *American Education*, (New York: McGraw-Hill, 2006), 160.

18. Sadker and Sadker, *Teachers, Schools, and Society*, 156–57.

19. Lisa Rivero, "The Unschool Mambo," at http://www.unschooling.com/library/index.shtml (accessed 27 January 2006), 3.

20. Sadker and Sadker, *Teachers, Schools, and Society*, 167.

14

Education of the Gifted and Talented

The idea that certain students have special talents that require teachers to modify their programs has been considered by educators since the formation of schools. Measuring students' abilities using intelligence tests or IQ scores can be traced back to at least 1916.[1] It was not until the 1950s that schools began to seriously consider developing special programs for students who were formally identified as being gifted or talented. This initiative was brought about in large part because of the perceived need to create more and better scientists and engineers. Especially after Sputnik and the onset of the Cold War, it was thought essential that we do a better job educating our most able students. This was considered necessary if we were to compete more effectively with the Union of Soviet Socialist Republics. The same reformers who were attacking progressive education during the fifties and early sixties were the ones who were highlighting this need. Included would be such people as Arthur Bestor, Jerome Bruner, James Conant, John Gardner, and Admiral Hyman Rickover.[2]

Although there were several efforts to stimulate gifted education during this time period, other topics eclipsed gifted education reform in the late sixties. It was not until 1978 when Congress passed the Gifted and Talented Children's Act that the issue again came to the forefront. The law stated the premise that "the nation's greatest resource for solving national problems in areas of national concern is its gifted and talented children."[3] Ten years later, Congress passed the Jacob K. Javits Gifted and Talented Act. Amended in 2001, the law described the gifted and talented as those students who "give evidence of high performance capability in areas such as intellectual, creative, artistic, or leadership capacity, or in special academic fields, and who require services or activities not ordinarily provided by the school in order to fully develop such capabilities."[4] This definition articulated a difference between those students who are gifted and those who are identified as talented. Gifted students were defined as those with "above-average intellectually ability," while talented children were those who demonstrated "excellence in drama, art, music, athletics, or leadership." It was noted that some students could be classified in just one of these categories while others might well be both gifted and talented.[5] Using these definitions, it was estimated that 10 to 20 percent of American students would qualify for special programs. Although this definition appears in federal legislation, states as well as individual school districts have also devised their own definitions.

One of the problems in the field of gifted and talented education is the difficulty educators face in determining which students should be eligible for special programs. While traditional IQ tests have often been a primary factor in identification, other information has also been considered. For example, a school might set a specific grade point average or require recommendations from teachers. One of the important individuals in this field is Joseph Ranzulli, who in 1978 identified three factors that should be evaluated to determine whether a student should be eligible for gifted and talented programs. These would include a student's "general ability (not necessarily 'superior') . . . task commitment (a motivational factor) and creativity."[6] In recent years the problem has been made even more complex with the introduction of Howard Gardner's theory of multiple intelligences. While traditional IQ tests might measure a student's ability to logically solve certain types of problems, Gardner and others believe that human intelligence includes varied skills and abilities. If judging one's intelligence is difficult, choosing students who have special talents can be an equally daunting task. Often music students are given special auditions while art students might have to present a portfolio of their work. Even with measures such as these, controversy in the selection process cannot be totally avoided. Many parents who are ambitious for their children can become critical of any selection procedure. This is true in part because participation in gifted and talented programs is for some a status symbol.

Even though there are difficulties in the selection process, there are strong arguments for offering special educational opportunities for these students. A study completed in 1996 concluded that:

> Gifted and talented students have much more complex needs than average and below average learners. . . . If these needs are not met, we now know that ability cannot be maintained; indeed, brain research tells us that ability will be lost. . . . When no programs are available to this group of learners a disservice is done, not only to these students, but to all society, as our finest minds not only lack nurture, they are wasted.[7]

Another argument for these programs can be found in research regarding school dropouts. Between 1962 and 1997, a study showed that between 15 and 20 percent of the students who had been identified as gifted dropped out of school. The reasons given for the high dropout rate included "boredom, some because of personal baggage, and some because of pregnancy." These were all students who had the potential to make positive contributions to their community and perhaps to the nation. Supporters of special programs argue that the absence of challenging educational alternatives is wasting our nation's talent reservoir.[8]

It is also possible that bored and frustrated students can become discipline problems in the classroom. It has also been suggested that not meeting the educational needs of these students can cause them to become withdrawn and depressed. As a result, they might be more likely to turn to alcohol and drugs or even a more drastic measure such as suicide. Perhaps the most often heard argument is that we spend billions of dollars for special education and remedial programs but very little to enhance the learning of the future leaders of their generation. Despite the fact that these appear to be persuasive arguments, as a nation we have not made a significant commitment to programs for the gifted and talented. This might be considered surprising, given the fact that the parents of these children are often successful and articulate members of their communities.

At the local level, when funds are short, the groups supporting athletics and music are usually much stronger than the parents seeking to begin or maintain a program for the gifted and talented. In establishing their priorities, many school districts have concluded that while special education and remedial programs are necessary, most gifted and talented students can make it on their own without additional help.

The fact is that even lacking significant amounts of outside money, schools have sought alternatives for enhancing the education of gifted and talented students. The oldest and perhaps most common approach can be labeled "acceleration." Since the concept of grade levels was introduced into the schools in the nineteenth century, some students have been allowed to skip whole grades. Today, many states encourage schools to allow more gifted students to skip individual classes at certain grade levels. For instance, a child moving into eighth grade would be allowed to skip eighth grade math or science and instead take ninth grade courses in those areas. Eleventh and twelfth grade students are allowed to meet some state requirements by taking college courses. Enrollment in advanced placement classes (college level courses) is increasing every year. Acceleration is also occurring under certain circumstances in music and in athletics. Any time a school uses this approach to challenge their more able students, the social implications must be considered. It is important that students being accelerated are able to function effectively with older classmates. Allowing students to move academically at their own pace is also possible in schools that have adopted a mastery approach to learning. Such a system divides the curriculum of a class into units and after a child demonstrates mastery (a high level of understanding) of a particular segment of the curriculum, these students are allowed to move ahead to the next unit even if their peers are still working on the previous unit.

Whether through mastery learning or the more traditional acceleration approaches, the fact remains that these students are still learning, in large measure, through the use of traditional teaching methods. If acceleration is the sole approach to accommodating gifted and talented children, it will not impact the future of progressive education.

A second method that has been adopted in some school districts does call upon progressive methods. Called "enrichment," the hope is to find ways to allow gifted students and perhaps other nongifted students to participate in in-depth experiences to enhance their understanding of the curriculum. These activities or projects are planned to encourage students to exercise problem-solving skills and to think creatively. For some time, the most common approach to enrichment is for the school to hire a teacher or teachers to "pull out" elementary or middle-school gifted children to a special room to work with other gifted children at their grade level. These small groups are given individual or group projects created to challenge them intellectually.

A teacher of the gifted and talented must do much more than give these students more of the same kind of homework that their classmates are doing. The goal is not to have the students do additional "busywork" but rather to provide them with a time during the school day when they will meet with other gifted students to become involved with more exciting and challenging work. Unfortunately, such pull-out programs are most likely to be found in wealthy suburban school districts that have enough money to support such a model. Even when school districts are able to hire teachers of the gifted and talented, because these programs are not mandated by the state or federal government, they will be on the list when budget cuts are considered. In any case, most American schools currently lack such pull-out programs. Because some communities see such offerings as being "elitist," they have chosen to hire an "enrichment teacher" whose job it is to create exciting enrichment lessons or units for every class in the school. In this way, all students benefit by being able to participate in an exciting and creative project. Unlike most acceleration options, gifted pull-out programs and special enrichment teachers do encourage teachers and schools to use progressive teaching techniques.

One final way schools are seeking to provide extra opportunities for their gifted and talented students is through out-of-school activities. Such opportunities have long been available for some of our most talented music and art students. Vocalists and instrumentalists are encouraged to compete in solo competitions or regional or statewide music ensembles. Art shows allow students to display their work and often compete with other students. Various competitions are common for academically gifted students. Some, unfortunately, are similar to trivial pursuit games or television quiz shows. In these academic competitions, student teams compete with rival schools in attempting to answer questions covering a variety of different subjects. Because of the nature of these competitions, the questions primarily involve recalling facts that students might have learned in school or picked up in their outside reading. Gifted students do gain recognition from these competitions for their broad knowledge and quick minds, but the approach has little to do with the objectives of progressive education.

One outside-of-school activity that is very much in keeping with progressive education theory is the Odyssey of the Mind program. Dr. Samuel Micklus, a college professor, created this unique competition in 1978.[9] Today, there are millions of students from around the world who participate. The international Odyssey of the Mind organization provides a specific problem each year for interested school groups. It might be one that requires the "students to build a structure that meets specific guidelines. . . . Another problem may require a theatrical solution that is written and performed by students. The problems are the same for all teams but the solutions vary based on the innovation of the students involved."[10] This is in keeping with the motto of the Odyssey of the Mind program, which is "Everybody is creative."[11] Frequently, a teacher or parent in the community will act as the advisor to a group of interested students. They will work together for weeks to prepare for the competition that begins at the local level with teams from other area schools. Winners continue by going on to regional and state contests. For a few lucky teams, there will also be a national and now an international competition. The most recent world finals held at the University of Maryland included seven hundred teams and drew fifteen thousand people.[12]

Whether or not progressive education theory will play a significant role in the future of gifted education will depend on a number of variables. The No Child Left Behind legislation seems to be primarily focused on remedial initiatives. The federal government and the states are now spending vast amounts of money to improve the test scores of our least able students. At the same time, both the president and Congress are now giving a significant amount of attention to the need of our country to quickly begin to prepare many more of our children for careers as scientists and engineers. A best-selling book, *The World is Flat*, by *New York Times* columnist Thomas L. Friedman, includes some alarming statistics. As he describes the effects of globalization, he highlights the fact that the United States has already lost many of its manufacturing and other unskilled and semiskilled jobs to foreign competition. For Friedman, the only way we can continue to compete in the world economy is for the United States to be the primary source for the new ideas that are so essential to succeeding in the world economy. We must have an abundance of creative brainpower in the areas of technology and science. This means our schools, colleges, and universities must prepare more quality scientists and engineers.

In his book he quoted the chairman of Intel as saying "for now, the United States still excels at teaching science and engineering at the graduate level, and also in university-based research." Although it is true that we may be ahead in these areas, China and India are currently producing many more technically trained workers; Friedman believes that if the current pace continues, China will catch up with us in a decade. He goes on quoting Chairman Barrett who has written, "We are not graduating the volume, we do not have a lock on the infrastructure, we do not have a lock on the new ideas and we are either flatlining, or in real dollars cutting back, our investments in physical science."[13] Many companies are already doing research and development in laboratories in other countries with scientists trained outside the United States. Harkening back to Sputnik and the *A Nation at Risk* report, Friedman points out that by the twelfth grade, students in the United States are still "hovering near the bottom in international tests related to math." Like many other critics, he blames teachers who are "turning off kids because they are not trained."[14] A number of critics have placed the blame on schools for the fact that our students do not seek careers in science and engineering.

The problem is not only that we are graduating many fewer scientists and engineers than in India and China but also that the percentage of scientific papers being published in leading journals is declining. For instance "the percentage of American papers published in the top physics journal, *Physical Review*, has fallen from 61 percent to 29 percent since 1983." It is also true that the U.S. government's "funding for research in physical and mathematical sciences and engineering, as a share of the GDP, actually declined by 37 percent between 1970 and 2004."[15]

This type of information has been stirring officials in Washington into action. Both the president and Congress are considering ways to stimulate increased student interest and achievement in the sciences. Whether it be through scholarship money for students, incentives for future science teachers, or allotting more money for research, the focus is again on our nation's need to create more engineers and scientists. Such initiatives are likely to influence schools to do more in the area of gifted education, especially as it relates to math and science.

It remains an open question whether these efforts will utilize progressive educational theory to reach this objective. The question is closely tied to the current focus on curriculum standards and testing programs. It is certainly possible to teach students in a way that encourages them to use their knowledge of math and science to solve problems in a creative way. While the lab portion of science classes can be designed to have students merely perform prepared exercises to prove what is taught in the classroom part of the course, another approach would be to create lab experiences that require students to find their own way to solve a science problem. Science classes and extracurricular activities related to science and math can be made less about preparing students to answer knowledge questions on a test and more about creative problem-solving using the scientific method. If this latter approach is integrated into the curriculum, as well as the examinations or other assessment methods, testmakers and teachers need to have students do more than "parrot back" what their textbooks and teachers have told them. Supporters of progressive education would argue that it is more essential than ever that we develop students who are problem-solvers. This is especially true for the gifted students, who are most likely to be our future scientists. They would agree with Friedman that this is necessary in order to successfully compete in what the author has called a "flat world."

There are many who are talking and writing about the need to alter the nation's current priorities of curriculum standards, high-stakes testing, and school accountability. A national debate is occurring in our school districts, state legislatures, and in Washington about the effectiveness of our current initiatives. Those who are opposed to the approach embodied in the No Child Left Behind legislation are making their opinions known in periodicals, books, and even in the courts. There is a core of modern-day progressive educators who have a different vision for our schools. We will now turn to the contemporary critics and examine what these progressive educators see as a more promising direction for our schools and also assess their likely impact on furthering the case for progressive education.

NOTES

1. Sally M. Reis, "Reflections on the Education of Gifted and Talented Students in the Twentieth Century: Milestones in the Development of Talent and Gifts in Young People," at http://www.gifted.uconn.edu/faculty/reis/publications/ Reflections_on_Major_Issues.htm (accessed 30 January 2006), 2.

2. Allan C. Ornstein, *Pushing the Envelope*, (Upper Saddle River, NJ: Merrill Prentice Hall, 2003), 258.

3. Peter H. Martorella, Candy M. Beal, and Cheryl Mason Bolick, *Teaching Social Studies in Middle and Secondary Schools*, (Upper Saddle River, NJ: Pearson, 2005), 373.

4. George S. Morrison, *Teaching in America*, (Boston: Pearson, 2006), 165–66.

5. Morrison, *Teaching in America*, 166.

6. Johanna K. Lemlech, *Curriculum and Instructional Methods for Elementary and Middle School*, (Upper Saddle River, NJ: Merrill, 1998), 14.

7. Jack L. Nelson, Stuart B. Palonsky, and Mary Rose McCarthy, *Critical Issues Education*, (New York: McGraw-Hill, 2004), 458.

8. Allan C. Ornstein, *Teaching and Schooling in America,* (Boston: Pearson Education Group, Inc., 2003), 349.

9. Sarah Ives, "Odyssey of the Mind's 'Wacky' World Finals," *National Geographic.com Kids* at http://news.nationalgeographic.com/kids/2004/05/odyssey ofmind.html (accessed 4 February 2006), 2.

10. "Extracurricular Activities," at http://www.mohonasen.org/03mohonhs/ hsextracurricular.htm (accessed 4 February 2006), 2.

11. "Odyssey of the Mind's 'Wacky' World Finals," 2.

12. "Odyssey of the Mind's 'Wacky' World Finals,"3.

13. Thomas L. Friedman, *The World is Flat*, (New York: Farrar, Strauss Giroux, 2005), 271.

14. Friedman, *The World is Flat*, 273.

15. Friedman, *The World is Flat*, 268–69.

15

Progressive Education Today

Despite the prevailing educational initiatives, which emphasize a return to traditional methods of teaching the basic subjects, state curriculum standards, high-stakes testing, and school accountability, there remain a number of vocal advocates of the theories associated with progressive education. There are also numerous schools scattered across the United States that are committed to the progressive education tradition. It is impossible to highlight all of these individuals and schools, but it is important to know that the ideas remain a part of our current educational scene. Most of these men and women are known within the education community, but their names and ideas for the most part are not widely recognized by the general public. Perhaps one of the better known critics of the current trends is Theodore Sizer.

A former headmaster of the Philips Andover Academy and dean of the Harvard Graduate School of Education, his book *Horace's Compromise* was published the same year as the release of the *A Nation at Risk* report. While conservative historian Diane Ravitch has characterized him as "the leading voice of American progressivism," his ideas cannot be considered radical. Still, he certainly has been critical of many of our current schools and has pointed to their "mediocre sameness." Even though Sizer has accepted many of the ideas of John Dewey, he does not, in Ravitch's words, "make a fetish of children's interest or disparage the importance of basic skills."[1] Like most progressives, he is convinced "that the purpose of education is not to transfer information from the brain of the teacher to the

brain of the students but to make students think. . . . Learning is primarily the responsibility of the student."[2] Sizer has not only written about
his ideas but also established an organization called the Coalition of Essential Schools. By the year 2000, Sizer's network had enlisted more
than 1,200 schools. The Coalition encourages schools to develop their
own reform plans based on the progressive goal of "the personalization
of learning."[3]

Another one of the modern-day champions of progressive schools is
Deborah Meier. She has led schools that were part of Theodore Sizer's
Coalition of Essential Schools. Although she is now in her midseventies,
Meier continues to be actively involved in the educational reform movement. Her long career encompasses experiences as a classroom teacher,
school administrator, teacher education professor, public speaker, and author. Perhaps her best-known contribution was the work that she did as an
administrator of a number of schools at East Harlem. From New York City
she has now moved on to the city of Boston, where she works in the role
of a principal. Despite this challenging position, she continues to speak
out against mandated standards and high-stakes testing.[4] For her, as it was
for Dewey, an essential outcome of schools should be to create "informed
citizens." To do so, Meier has written that students must develop five
"habits of mind." These "habits of mind" cause well-educated citizens to
raise the following questions.

- How do you know what you know? (Evidence)
- From whose viewpoint is this being presented? (Perspective)
- How is this event or work connected to others? (Connections)
- What if things were different? (Supposition)
- Why is this important? (Relevance)[5]

Deborah Meier is also a proponent of smaller, self-governing schools. She
has written "that every school must have the power and the responsibility
to select and design its own particulars."[6] For her, "top-down" reforms
such as those required by the No Child Left Behind legislation are
doomed to failure. In her work in New York and Boston, she established
smaller schools where the principal is a "head teacher." The schools rely
on the creative ideas of teachers who are able to establish a "family-like"
setting in their school.

Perhaps even more squarely in the progressive tradition than either Theodore Sizer or Deborah Meier is the former National Teacher of the Year, Dennis Littky. Following his long career as a classroom teacher, Littky became a school administrator who now leads the Rhode Island Regional Career and Technical Center. As cofounder of the school that is commonly known as The Met, Littky has introduced a truly progressive plan for the school. The Met is made up of six separate buildings, each with its own principal and approximately one hundred students. These schools operate without required classes, tests, or grades. It is the goal of the school "to take one-student-at-a-time." The program works as follows:

> Each student works with a teacher—known at The Met as an "advisor"—to put together an individualized curriculum depending on his or her interests. There's little in the way of standard coursework: students devise independent projects and their progress is closely monitored throughout the semester by their advisors, peers, parents, and internship mentors.

> Each advisor works with about fifteen students, staying with the same group throughout the four years of high school. While that means faculty members don't specialize in particular areas, it does foster a tie between teacher and student that is extraordinary for a public high school, and that is an integral part of the Met's educational philosophy.[7]

In the progressive tradition, Littky believes that schools should focus "on students' individual interests and fostering their curiosity, research and communication skills."[8]

Despite the fact that The Met is an inner-city school, with 65 percent of its students qualifying for federal meal subsidies, the academic results of the school are much higher than might be expected. The attendance and graduation rates are both approximately 94 percent, which places The Met's students among the best in the state. Students from the school have been accepted by such institutions as the University of Chicago and Brown University. One hundred percent of the graduates have been accepted into a college. As a result of his success in Providence, Rhode Island, Littky was able to obtain a grant from the Bill and Melinda Gates Foundation to begin similar schools throughout the nation. As of February 2006, twenty-four schools based on the Littky model are already functioning. The goal is to expand to fifty-four such schools in the near future.[9]

Dennis Littky's new progressive schools will merely add to the number of similar institutions, many of which have been in existence since the beginning of the progressive education movement. One such institution is the School of Organic Education, which was originally founded by Marietta Johnson in 1907.

> Johnson's philosophy of education was based on the premise that a child is a growing organism, and that growth cannot be forced but must unfold naturally within the organism itself. Schools, therefore, should provide the most ideal environment possible in which the child can be nourished and nurtured toward physical, mental, and emotional health. She believed that the imposition of external standards produced self-consciousness and stifled the natural learning process.[10]

The school located in Fairhope, Alabama, operates on the assumption that "play is the child's work," and thus "in the unstructured atmosphere of The School of Organic Education, kids are creative, motivated learners."[11]

A school similar to The School of Organic Education is the Presidio Hill School in San Francisco. Founded in 1918, it continues today as an example of a school committed to progressive education theory. Believing that "no two children learn the same way," the K–8 program at Presidio emphasizes student projects, cross-curricular activities, service learning, field trips, art, music, drama, and poetry.[12]

Beginning the same year as the Presidio Hill School, the Carson Valley School in Philadelphia, Pennsylvania, began its long history as the Carson College for Orphan Girls. Its first president, Elsa Ueland, was a student of both John Dewey and Maria Montessori. In a history of the school, "Philadelphia's Progressive Orphanage," author David R. Contosta writes that the school is "an institutional embodiment of progressivism." Beginning as a facility for orphan girls, the school now offers an open enrollment policy. Its early history illustrates clearly the relationship between the progressive education movement and the progressive social and political causes that were prominent in the United States at the beginning of the twentieth century.[13]

Also in Pennsylvania, on a beautiful wooded campus, one can find the School in Rose Valley. Founded in 1929, it is an elementary school that also includes a preschool program. It advertises "a hands-on, child-centered education." The goal of the school is to develop in its students "problem-solving skills," the ability to "think independently, work collaboratively, and communicate effectively." That the school is still an active leader in fostering the progressive tradition of education can be seen by its sponsorship of a yearlong symposium for progressive educators in 2004–2005. The keynote speaker at the Spring conference was Alfie Kohn.[14]

Kohn's 1999 book, *The Schools Our Children Deserve*, has the subtitle "Moving Beyond Traditional Classrooms and Tougher Standards." About this book, Jonathan Kozol wrote that Kohn "draws upon a rich tradition, citing the work of Dewey, Bruner, and Holt, among others, but he now takes his proper place within their ranks. In short, this is a remarkable book that should become a classic in the field." Theodore Sizer wrote about the same book that "in this lively, provocative, and well-researched book, Alfie Kohn provides a needed antidote to current official education policy."[15] Kohn is an outspoken advocate of progressive education on many fronts. In an article published in the *Washington Post* he wrote the following.

> The best kind of teaching takes its cue from the understanding that people are active learners. In such a classroom, students are constantly making decisions, becoming participants in their own education. Each is part of a community of learners, coming to understand ideas from the inside out with one another's help. They still acquire facts and skills, but in a context, and for a purpose. Their questions drive the curriculum. Learning to think like scientists and historians matters more than memorizing lists of definitions and dates.[16]

For him, "learning is a process in which the words discovery, exploration, and curiosity are found in abundance." He is a believer that the teacher's role is to engage students and to help them gain "deeper understanding." Like Dewey, Kohn believes that students should be allowed to make mistakes as they are "invaluable clues as to how the student is thinking, and second, because to do so creates a climate that ultimately promotes more successful learning." For him it is all right for students to be "confused" and even to fall on their faces during the learning process. The key to his thinking is that "students are not receptacles to be filled with knowledge or clay to be molded. They, like all of us, are active meaning-makers." The role of the teacher is "to develop curriculum with the students in mind, and not traditional education norms." The curriculum should be shaped in part by student interest and must allow children to find "answers to their own questions."[17]

Another influential contemporary author in the progressive tradition is Herbert Kohl. Kohl, who has spent his professional life as a classroom teacher, speaks as one who for years has sought in his own classroom to find the best approach to education. Since the 1960s, in his more than forty books, he has become an influential writer in the field of education. Known as the "founder of the Open School Movement, Kohl has never been timid about suggesting an overhaul of the traditional system." While he adamantly agrees that schools must teach the basic skills, he believes that it is equally important "not only to engage students' imagination, but also to convince them that they are people of worth who can do something in a very difficult world."[18]

According to Kohl, teachers need to "respect the unique way a child perceives the world, and accordingly shape the way a child is going to learn." In doing so, it is important to "respect the learner as a person who is connected to a family, the world, and the larger things in life."[19] A practical teacher, he wrote in the Introduction to his 1998 book, *The Discipline of Hope*, that:

> I want students to explore learning through doing, but also through reflection and hard study. I want them to learn hard skills in soft ways. Most of all, I want my students, wherever I teach, to feel part of a compassionate learning community where they are honored as individuals, where they respect each other, and where they respect and love learning itself.[20]

Perhaps even more upset with the current focus of schools than Herbert Kohl is the Stanford professor Elliot W. Eisner. Like many others, he argues that "the point of learning anything in school is not primarily to enable one to do well in school—although most parents and students believe this to be the case—it is to enable one to do well in life." For Eisner, the reason for learning is to "enable one to produce the questions and perform the activities that one's outside life will require." To do this, schools should seek to create in their students "intrinsic motivation" and joy in learning, as opposed to a "lust for point accumulation."[21] The role of schools is to assist students in gradually developing "increased responsibility for framing their own goals and learning. . . . We want students eventually to become the architects of their own education. The long-term aim of teaching is to make it unnecessary."[22]

In a 2005 article in the magazine *Educational Leadership*, Eisner wrote that "progressive educators gave us a vision of the whole child. Where has that vision gone now that we need it most?"[23] In answering this question he blames "standardization," which "takes place as states define expectations and . . . holds schools and those who work in them accountable for the results." In a section of the article entitled "A Vision Revived," he writes that when one compares a progressive classroom in any era with the dull routine found in most classrooms today, we see that the vision is one that we need more than ever. For him, our current "measurement mania" that is fostered by high-stakes testing is causing schools and teachers to forget the fundamental goal of preparing students to become caring, creative, and useful people and citizens.[24]

Nel Noddings, a final example of a modern-day progressive, has attempted to define what professor Eisner was referring to when he wrote about the "whole child." In an article in the September 2005 issue of *Educational Leadership*, she criticizes the No Child Left Behind law for failing to deal with what for her are the three most basic questions relating to a child's education. These include the following.

- What are the proper aims of education?
- How can public schools serve a democratic society?
- What does it mean to educate the whole child?[25]

Early in the twentieth century, a major study listed the following as the appropriate goals for answering the third question defining the whole child. These goals are as follows: (1) health; (2) command of the fundamental processes; (3) worthy home membership; (4) vocation; (5) citizenship; (6) worthy use of leisure; and (7) ethical character. Noddings adds the additional goal of happiness. She points out that "great thinkers have associated happiness with such qualities as a rich intellectual life, rewarding human relationships, love of home and place, sound character, good parenting, spirituality, and a job that one loves." It is her view that schools can help students to understand these components of happiness, at least in part, by making "classrooms genuinely happy places."[26] Along with the attempt to create happy children, Noddings would argue that teachers must "address moral, social, emotional and aesthetic questions with respect and sensitivity when they arise."[27] Noddings is considered in one standard educational textbook as a major voice for progressivism. The textbook's author quotes Noddings as saying that "an ethic of care can best be cultivated when the curriculum is centered around the interest of students" and that schools must seek "to nourish the physical, spiritual, occupational, and intellectual development of each child."[28]

Noddings, along with other contemporary progressives, is uncomfortable with the seemingly narrow goals of the current educational initiatives. She worries that, as a nation, we are so focused on raising test scores that our schools are ignoring the broader and more important goals of education. Like the progressive educators in earlier eras, modern-day progressives have differences as to the proper way to reform the current reality. At the same time, they are unanimous in the view that our present direction in education is misguided.

Several observations can be made about the current progressive critics. First, it is unfortunately true that none of those mentioned in this chapter are young people. As we proceed further into the twenty-first century, it will be necessary that new voices emerge to articulate the virtues of progressive educational theory. One might guess that this new generation of progressive educators will indeed emerge as products of our current teacher education programs. Whether this will occur remains to be seen. Secondly, it must be admitted that none of the individuals mentioned in this chapter have risen to a position of national prominence. Their articles and books are read in large part by those already involved in the field of education. On the other hand, their voices, along with those of journalists and a number of political leaders, have stimulated a national debate over the current course of educational reform in this country. There is no question that the conflict between the proponents of traditional education theory and practices and its critics has never been more spirited. In the final chapter, it would now seem appropriate to summarize where we are and what might become of the future of progressive education in America.

NOTES

1. Diane Ravitch, *Left Back*, (New York: Simon and Schuster, 2000), 418–419.

2. Edward B. Fiske, *Smart Schools, Smart Kids*, (New York: Simon and Schuster, 1992), 66–67.

3. Myra Pollack Sadker and David Miller Sadker, *Teachers, Schools, and Society*, (Boston: McGraw Hill, 2000), 262.

4. "Deborah Meier," at www.pbs.org/kcet/publicschool/innovators/meier.html (accessed 15 February 2006), 1.

5. Barry S. Kogan, ed., *Common Schools, Uncommon Futures*, (New York: Teachers College Press, 1997), 61.

6. James Wm. Noll, ed., *Taking Sides*, (Guilford, CT: McGraw-Hill/Dushkin, 2004), 327.

7. "Dennis Littky: Innovation in Education, One Student at a Time," *Business Inventory Factory* at http://www.businessinventoryfactory.com/index.php (accessed 16 February 2006), 1.

8. "Dennis Littky: Innovation in Education, One Student at a Time," 2.

9. "Innovation in Education, One Student at a Time," at http://www.riedc .com/riedc/blue_sky/32/433/ (accessed 17 Februray 2006), 3.

10. Crysta Kessler, "Play is the Child's Work: In the Unstructured Atmosphere of the School of Organic Education, Kids Are Creative, Motivated Learners," at http://www.findarticles.com/p/articles/mi_m0838/id_130/ai_n1374199/print (accessed 17 February 2006), 1.

11. "Play is the Child's Work: In the Unstructured Atmosphere of the School of Organic Education, Kids Are Creative, Motivated Learners," 1.

12. "A Progressive School," at http://www.presidiohill.org/about/archives/ 205/06/our_mission_sta.php (accessed 8 February 2006), 2.

13. "Philadelphia's Progressive Orphanage," at http://www.psupress.org/ books/titles/0-271-01714-7.html (accessed 18 November 2005), 1.

14. "Progressive Education in the 21st Century," at http://www.theschoolin rosevalley.org/symposium.asp (accessed 8 February 2006), 1.

15. Alfie Kohn, *The Schools Our Children Deserve*, (New York: Houghton Mifflin, 1999) inside cover.

16. Alfie Kohn, "A LOOK AT . . . Getting Back to Basics: First Lesson: Unlearn How We Learned," 10 October 1999, at *Washington Post* at www.alfiekohn .org/teaching/alagbtb.htm, (accessed 14 March 2005), 3.

17. Joseph Milnes, "The Educational Theory of Alfie Kohn," at http://www .newfoundations.com/GALLERY/Kohn.html (accessed 15 February 2006), 1–2.

18. Marge Scherer, "Creating a Positive Classroom; A Conversation with Herb Kohl" at http://www.nea.org/taeachexperience/tsklk040621.html (accessed 17 February, 2006), 1.

19. Marge Scherer, "Creating a Positive Classroom; A Conversation with Herb Kohl," 6.

20. Herbert Kohl, *The Discipline of Hope*, (New York: Simon and Schuster, 1998).

21. Kevin Ryan and James M. Cooper, *Kaleidoscope*, (Boston: Houghton Mifflin Company, 2004), 371.

22. Ryan and Cooper, *Kaleidoscope*, 272.

23. Elliot Eisner, "Back to Whole," *Educational Leadership*, September 2005, 63, no. 1 at http://ascd.org/portal/site/ascd/template.MAXIMIZE/menuitem (accessed 9 September 2005), 1.

24. Eisner, "Back to Whole," 4–5.

25. Nel Noddings, "What Does It Mean to Educate the Whole Child?" *Educational Leadership*, September 2005, 63, no. 1 at http://www.ascd.org/authors/ed_lead/e1200509_noddings.html (accessed 2 February 2006), 1.

26. Noddings, "What Does It Mean to Educate the Whole Child?," 2.

27. Noddings, "What Does It Mean to Educate the Whole Child?," 4.

28. Myra Pollack Sadker and David Miller Sadker, *Teachers, Schools, and Society*, (Boston: McGraw Hill, 2003), 367.

16

The Future of Progressive Education

What David J. Ferrero has called "the 100 Years War between 'progressives' and 'traditionalists'" continues unabated in the twenty-first century. Undoubtedly, the current initiatives in public education favor those who support the traditional approach. It is equally true that many critics believe that inflexible state curriculum standards enforced by high-stakes tests are restricting teachers' flexibility in employing methods other than teacher-centered direct instruction. Teachers at all levels are worried about "covering" the states' curriculum standards. It is likely that they are also concerned about losing class time if they plan projects, debates, or field trips. Our nation's ongoing poor showing in comparative international tests continues to create pressure to concentrate on the type of instruction that traditionalists believe will be most effective in raising test scores.

At the federal level, the president has proposed extending mandatory testing beyond grade eight into the high school. There are also renewed discussions about the possibility of establishing national curriculum standards and tests. These would replace the current curriculum objectives and examinations that are being prepared at the state level. Supporters of such a plan point to the differences between how states are enforcing the requirement to provide specific curriculum standards in every basic subject. They also point out that the mandatory tests being given by the states vary greatly. National standards outlining what students should know and be able to do in every subject area, along with national tests on these standards, would make it much easier to compare the education students are receiving in every school district in the country. States with poor results on national tests could more easily be targeted for remedial measures. The fact that many countries that have done well in international tests do have national curriculums and tests is also referenced in making the case for nationalizing curriculum and testing.

Although attempts during the Clinton years to develop a national social studies curriculum failed, it is possible that new efforts may be undertaken by the federal government as the nation becomes frustrated by the lack of adequate gains in international tests. If the United States chooses such a course of action, it is very possible that schools and teachers will have even less flexibility in using progressive education theory and methods. Looking ahead, it is easy for progressives to become discouraged about the future.

Still, there are reasons to believe that while we are currently experiencing a swing of the educational pendulum to the right, that inevitably it will move back again in a direction that is more favorable to progressive education. Certainly as we have seen, it would be premature to declare the final decline of progressive education in the United States. The growing popularity of the Montessori method, especially at the preschool and primary level, signals that there is a market for schools that emphasize creativity and "learning by doing."

The idea of school choice, in all of its many manifestations, is also allowing parents to choose schools established in the progressive tradition. Unfortunately, a significant number of the parents selecting Montessori schools and progressive schools of choice can be described as white middle- and upper-class liberals. Although their number is still relatively small compared to the entire population, many of these parents tend to be active and vocal in their school district. There is also reason to surmise that growing numbers of urban minorities are looking to choice as a way to escape what they perceive as schools that are failing to properly educate their children.

Perhaps an even more important factor in ensuring the continued survival of progressive education is the role being played by our teacher education programs. As we have seen in almost every class and textbook experienced by future teachers, there are discussions of the need to use a variety of teaching techniques. The introduction of the inclusion of special education students into regular classrooms, along with the decline of academic grouping, is creating in most classrooms a greater diversity of students than we have seen in recent years. Approaches such as nongraded classrooms and diversification of instruction are commonly discussed in teacher education programs. Cooperative learning and the use of projects are frequently used in teacher education classes. It is hard to believe that these college experiences will not at least in some way affect the teaching methods used by the graduates of their programs.

Middle-school theory, which has been popular during the past fifty years, also calls for a more student-centered program that is designed especially for this age group. Advocates of middle schools call for more active learning methods as opposed to teacher lectures. Curricular and extracurricular programs, according to theory, should be based more on the developmental level of the children. It is true that not all middle schools are serious about the theory and that many still resemble traditional junior high schools. There is also the possibility that the current emphasis on testing may push others in this direction. Even if this occurs, most educators have accepted the idea that middle-school students are different than high-school students and that their educational programs should be more student-centered.

Some opportunities for gifted and talented students also emphasize more academic freedom for those children admitted to these programs. An example, as we have noted, would be the Odyssey of the Mind program, which stimulates students' creative problem-solving skills. Certainly, this extracurricular activity would be applauded by the supporters of progressive education. The current initiative to develop many more scientists and engineers also has the potential of infusing additional and imaginative laboratory exercises into our science classes.

Finally, although no twenty-first-century John Dewey has emerged, there continue to be a significant number of individuals who are very vocal in their criticisms of the current direction of education. It should be noted that some of these critics are outside of the education profession. The most common criticism of the current initiatives comes from those worried about high-stakes testing. In an article appearing in the liberal newsmagazine, *The Nation,* in June 2000, the authors noted that:

> Despite the political popularity of the testing "solution," many educators and civil rights advocates are suggesting that it has actually exacerbated the

problems it sought to alleviate. They claim that these policies discriminate against minority students, undermine teachers, reduce opportunities for students to engage in creative and complex learning assignments, and deny high school diplomas because of students' failure to pass subjects they were never taught. They argue that using tests to raise academic standards makes as much sense as relying upon thermometers to reduce fevers. Most compellingly, they maintain that these tests are directing sanctions against the victims, rather than the perpetrators of educational inequities. [1]

A research project conducted by Audrey L. Amrein and David C. Berliner was summarized in the magazine *Educational Leadership* in 2003. It lists what the researchers found are the negative results of high-stakes testing:

- Rather than increasing student motivation, they believe that the tests cause students to "become less intrinsically motivated to learn and less likely to engage in critical thinking." Teachers, on the other hand, choose to "take greater control of the learning experiences of their students," which denies them the possibility of directing "their own learning."
- It is the conclusion of the study that high-stakes testing is one factor causing an increased dropout rate in the United States. This in turn is leading more students to seek alternative diplomas, such as the so-called GED (General Education Diploma). This degree is based totally on passing tests.
- There is increased grade retention occurring and this, in turn, it is argued, has caused more students to drop out of school.
- Schools are spending valuable time teaching test-taking techniques and teaching only content that is likely to appear on the test.[2]

In the same issue of *Educational Leadership* magazine, Monty Neill urges educators to repudiate tests that narrow the curriculum and to "focus instead on formative assessment practices that encourage skilled teaching and high level learning."[3]

It is not only in educational periodicals where our current reliance on testing has been attacked. Books are being published that argue that the approach is a negative one. In a 1999 book entitled *Standardized Minds*, Peter Sacks has written that "test-driven classrooms exacerbate boredom, fear, and lethargy, promoting all manner of mechanical behaviors on the part of teachers, students, and schools, and bleed schoolchildren of their natural love of learning."[4]

Even before the passage of the No Child Left Behind Act, Alfie Kohn wrote a book titled *The Case Against Standardized Testing*. The subtitle of the book was "Raising the Scores, Ruining the Schools." Kohn makes the argument that:

- High scores often signify relatively superficial thinking.
- Many of the leading tests were never intended to measure teaching or learning.
- A school that improves its test results may well have lowered its standards to do so.
- Far from helping to "close the gap," the use of standardized testing is most damaging for low-income and minority students
- As much as 90 percent of the variations in test scores among schools or states have nothing to do with quality instruction.
- Far more meaningful measures of student learning—or school quality—are available.[5]

A third book that deals with the negative aspects of testing is titled *High Stakes: Children, Testing, and the Failure in American Schools*. In this book, the authors, Dale D. Johnson and Bonnie Johnson, tell of their work during one year in a rural school district. For them, the experience demonstrated the "tyranny and oppression" that high-stakes testing and accountability was creating in a small, poor school district. They believe that "there is growing opposition to the accountability movement and especially to high-stakes testing" in schools all over America.[6]

Throughout our history, the education sections in libraries and bookstores have been filled with volumes criticizing education in the United States. Despite its many critics, No Child Left Behind continues to have many supporters, and there is a significant number of people who associate any form of progressive education as being negative. For instance, one conservative website, www.speakout.com, includes this sentence in an article dealing with the legacy of progressive education: "We probably would be better off if Dewey and his ilk had peddled their intellectual wares elsewhere, perhaps in Dewey's beloved Soviet Union."[7] Another typical view is expressed in the publication of the Hoover Institution that states "school reformers today are still trying to put into effect the turn-of-the-century progressive ideas of John Dewey and others. These ideas were largely misguided one hundred years ago, and they are largely misguided now."[8]

With this type of angry opposition and because so many of the current members of Congress voted for the No Child Left Behind law, change will be difficult. The law is not likely to be dramatically altered when it is considered for reauthorization in 2007. For the past several years, the most frequent criticism by Democrats is not about the initiatives created by the law but rather the failure of the Bush Administration to properly fund it. As a result, it is difficult to see in this decade that as a nation we will totally turn away from curriculum standards, high-stakes testing, and school accountability. At the same time, the current Secretary of Education, Margaret Spellings, has become significantly more flexible in the enforcement of the law. Unlike her predecessor Rod Paige, she has been somewhat sensitive to the criticisms by teachers' unions, state legislatures, and individual school districts. With various provisions to the law currently being challenged in the courts, it is also possible that enforcement will be affected by judicial decisions. Still, it is likely that Secretary Spellings will bend only so far. She has been quoted as saying "As we say in Texas, if all you ever do is all you've ever done, then all you'll ever get is all you ever got—And all we ever got is really not good enough."[9]

Undoubtedly the fierce debates about the law will continue and will affect educational decisions at every level. Especially in Washington, one can expect that with the urging and support of the teachers' unions, a victorious Democratic party might be expected to spend more money on public education if it is able to control Congress as a result of the 2006 election. A Democratic Congress also is likely to be less sympathetic with choice options, especially vouchers involving nonpublic schools. Whether the Democrats would attempt a major overhaul of the No Child Left Behind law is difficult to predict. There is no question that many people in the educational community have serious reservations about the initiatives created by the law, but the general public is not yet nearly as critical.

It is nearly impossible to predict how politics will affect the future of progressive education. Chances are likely that school choice will continue to give parents some opportunities to select progressive education options for their children. Even if choice is expanded and we have more progressive schools in this country, it will still be a small minority of our students who are being exposed to this approach. There is another possible path that might be followed that would bring progressive methods into the mainstream of all of our public schools. If this were to happen, there must first be some kind of truce between traditionalists and progressives as well as an acceptance of the idea that both approaches can be used in every classroom.

That such an accommodation is indeed possible can be seen in the history of the decades-old struggle between those who supported a traditional phonics-based reading program and the advocates of whole language. Today many elementary schools have adopted reading programs that include methods associated with both approaches. In these classrooms, teachers may be using the traditional basal readers and having students learn spelling words each week out of a separate book. They are also emphasizing a phonetic approach to identifying and pronouncing words that are new to the children. At the same time, these teachers are employing such whole-language techniques as using context clues to identify words, using classic childhood literature in the form of big books, utilizing a classroom library that is used to encourage children to read on their own, and perhaps taking spelling words and vocabulary from the books being read in class. Such a combined approach appears to be very popular in many schools.

Compromise can also occur in the field of social studies. There is little argument that students need to know key names and dates in history or that they should be acquainted with the major provisions of the U.S. Constitution. Teachers do have to be purveyors of information. At the same time, if adequate flexibility is accorded to teachers, there is no reason that an American history teacher could not give his or her students the opportunity to research the arguments that were prevalent at the time the Constitution was being ratified. The class could be divided between the Federalists and Antifederalists and following a time of individual and group research, a town meeting simulation could be held to debate whether the community should favor ratification of the proposed Constitution. Students would likely better remember what they learned as they were engaged in such an active learning experience. Obviously, every controversy being studied in social studies class cannot involve individual research and formal debates, but if such progressive techniques were encouraged, it is very possible that many students would find school more interesting.

Of course to allow teachers to use such progressive teaching techniques, it would necessitate that the assessment instruments used by schools become more flexible. There would have to be less reliance on factual objective tests and more opportunities for creative answers to essay questions. An example of a question that would allow a student to use his or her experience in the debate described above would be "Using a conflict situation in American history, identify the problem, give the primary arguments dealing with the issue, and explain and justify your own position on the problem." Social studies classes can also include experiences in service learning that would allow students to spend volunteer hours in the community engaged in useful work. Such an activity can be assessed using something other than tests. The student can develop a portfolio or a journal that records his or her reactions to the learning experience. In choosing projects, students could be given the opportunity to follow their own interests, which is another important goal of progressive education theory.

Similar progressive educational techniques could also be more prominent in other classes. In science and math, if we are serious that we wish to develop truly creative problem solvers, these classes must include laboratories and lessons that offer such opportunities to students. It will not be enough to have them memorize their math and science textbooks in order to pass short-answer tests. At least some of the science labs should have as a goal giving students the opportunity to creatively solve problems.

English teachers can also utilize student interests in writing exercises and in the research topics that they assign to students. Children at all ages should be given the opportunity to act out plays and to write creatively about the literature they are exposed to. Multidisciplinary projects that have students combining several subjects, including technology, in solving a problem, also can be encouraged in our schools. In carrying out such projects, teachers would in the progressive tradition, be advisors or facilitators of learning rather than just information givers.

All of these approaches are possible if we can make the appropriate accommodations with the current emphasis on very specific curriculum requirements, high-stakes testing, and accountability. Even traditional educators should be able to accept the progressive goals expressed by Herbert Berlak, which are "to engage the learner, nurture imagination," to stimulate "cognitive and artistic expression and foster social-emotional and moral development."[10] Many people would agree with S. Counts when he wrote that:

> In the minds of most Americans, the Progressive Education movement, in spite of its complexity, does stand for certain rather definite things. Moreover, few would deny that it has a number of large achievements to its credit. It has focused attention squarely upon the child; it has recognized the fundamental importance of the interest of the learner; it has defended the thesis that activity lies at the root of all true education; it has conceived learning in terms of life situations and growth of character; it has championed the rights of the child as a free personality.[11]

Whether progressive education continues to be primarily an option for a limited number of students or becomes increasingly integrated in the mainstream remains to be seen. Still, we can conclude that although its influence may currently be at a low ebb in the United States, it will remain a force that will continue to influence our schools. The final word in this review of progressive education will be given to John Dewey, who ended his book *Experience and Education* with his "firm belief" that:

> the fundamental issue is not of new versus old education nor of progressive against traditional education but a question of what anything whatever must be to be worthy of the name education. I am not, I hope and believe, in favor of any ends or any methods simply because the name progressive may be applied to them. . . . What we want and need is education pure and simple, and we shall make sure and faster progress when we devote ourselves to finding out just what education is and what conditions have to be satisfied in order that education may be a reality and not a name or a slogan.[12]

NOTES

1. Gary Orfield and Johanna Wald, "Testing, Testing," *The Nation*, 5 June 2000, 38.

2. Audrey L. Amrein and David C. Berliner, "The Effects of High-Stakes Testing on Student Motivation and Learning," *Educational Leadership*, February 2003, 60, no. 5, 32–33.

3. Amrein and Berliner, "The Effects of High-Stakes Testing on Student Motivation and Learning," 43.

4. Peter Sacks, *Standardized Minds*, (Cambridge, MA: Perseus Publishing, 1999), 256–57.

5. Alfie Kohn, *The Case Against Standardized Testing*, (Portsmouth, NH: Heinemann, 2000), back cover.

6. Dale D. Johnson and Bonnie Johnson, *High Stakes: Children, Testing, and the Failure in American Schools*, (Lanham, MD: Roman & Littlefield, Inc., 2002), xix.

7. Jerry Jesness, "The Legacy of Progressive Education," at www.speakout .com/activism/opinion/2971-1.html (accessed 10 February 2006), 1.

8. Williamson M. Evers, "How Progressive Education Gets It Wrong," *Hoover Institution*, at http://www.hooverdigest.org/984/evers.html, (accessed 15 February 2006), 1.

9. "Spellings More Flexible on NCLB Law," at http://www.cnn.com/2006/ EDUCATION/01/19/SPELLINGS.INTERVIEW.AP/INDEX.HTML (accessed 19 January 2006), 3.

10. Harold Berlak, "The *No Child Left Behind Act* and the Assault on Progressive Education and Local Control" at http://www.pipeline.com/~rougeforum/PolicyandNCLB.htm (accessed 17 May 2005), 1.

11. George S. Counts, "Dare Progressive Education Be Progressive?" at http://courses.wccnet.edu/play/cls2002/counts.htm (accessed 15 February 2006), 1.

12. L. Glen Smith and Joan K. Smith, *Lives in Education*, (New York: St. Martin's Press, 1994), 294.

About the Author

William Hayes has been a high-school social studies teacher, department chair, assistant principal, and principal. From 1973–1994, he served as superintendent of schools for the Byron-Bergen Central School District, located eighteen miles west of Rochester, New York. During his career, he was an active member of the New York State Council of Superintendents and is the author of a council publication, *The Superintendency: Thoughts for New Superintendents*, which is used to prepare new superintendents in New York State.

Mr. Hayes has also written a number of articles for various educational journals. After retiring from the superintendency, he served as chair of the Teacher Education Division at Roberts Wesleyan College in Rochester, New York, until 2003. He currently remains a full-time teacher at Roberts Wesleyan. During the past five years he has written nine books that have all been published by Scarecrow Education Press and Rowman & Littlefield Education: *Real-Life Case Studies for School Administrators*; *Real-Life Case Studies for Teachers*; *So You Want to be a Superintendent?*; *So You Want to be a School Board Member?*; *Real-Life Case Studies for School Board Members*; *So You Want to Become a College Professor?*; *So You Want to Become a Principal?*; *Are We Still a Nation at Risk Two Decades Later?*; and *Horace Mann's Vision of the Public Schools: Is it Still Relevant?*